Wilfried Huchzermeyer

Sri Aurobindo
and
European Philosophy

edition sawitri

Karlsruhe

ACKNOWLEDGEMENTS

Unless otherwise indicated all quotations and photographs of the Mother and Sri Aurobindo are copyright of the Sri Aurobindo Ashram Trust, Pondicherry, reproduced here with acknowledgements and thanks to the Trustees.

Sri Aurobindo and European Philosophy
Copyright : Verlag W. Huchzermeyer
Author : Verlag W. Huchzermeyer

ISBN: 978-93-95460-39-2 (eBook)
ISBN: 978-93-95460-87-3 (Print)

BISAC Code:
PHI035000, PHILOSOPHY / Essays
PHI004000, PHILOSOPHY / Epistemology
EDU042000, EDUCATION / Essays
PHI003000, PHILOSOPHY / Eastern

Thema Subject Category:
Q, Philosophy and Religion
QRA, Religion: general

Cataloging-in-Publication Data for this title is available from the Library of Congress.

Published by:
PRISMA, an imprint of Digital Media Initiatives
PRISMA, Aurelec/ Prayogshala,
Auroville 605101, Tamil Nadu, India
www.prisma.haus

CONTENTS

Preface	8
1. THE LIFE DIVINE	10
Sri Aurobindo's philosophy	10
Supermind	12
The psychic being	13
2. HERACLITUS – BEING AND BECOMING	15
Thunderbolt and fire	16
Sri Aurobindo's commentary	18
The idea of evolution	19
The Logos	22
Criticism	24
3. PLATO – THE THEORY OF IDEAS	27
Plato's theory of ideas	28
Sri Aurobindo's Real-Idea	29
The differences	31
K.D. Sethna's analysis	32
4. PLOTINUS AND THE *NOUS*	38
Plotinus' life and philosophy	41
The *Nous* with Anaxagoras	44
The Gnosis	45
5. SCHELLING AND HIS NATURAL PHILOSOPHY	48
Schelling's life and work	50
Schelling's Indian studies	52
The evolutionary philosophy of Sri Aurobindo	54
Schelling's natural philosophy	58
Real-Idealism	62
Evil and the anti-divine	66
Sri Aurobindo on the anti-divine	67

6. HEGEL AND THE ABSOLUTE IDEALISM	72
The philosophy of "aufheben"	74
Critique of dialectical reasoning	76
Hegel's philosophy	78
World-spirit and world-history	80
S.K. Maitra's critique of Hegel	82
Steve Odin's comparative study	85
Sri Aurobindo's philosophy of history	89
7. NIETZSCHE AND THE IDEAL OF SUPERMAN	94
Superman in Sri Aurobindo's main works	96
R. Safranski's portrait of Nietzsche	100
Zarathustra and Superman	106
Hirschberger's criticism and résumé	109
8. BERGSON AND THE INTUITION	112
Sri Aurobindo's commentaries	114
Intuition and Consciousness-Force	115
S.K. Maitras comparative study	118
Evolution	120
Sri Aurobindo on Time	123
9. TEILHARD DE CHARDIN AND THE OMEGA-POINT	127
Teilhard's philosophy	129
Comparative studies	132
F.J. Korom's study	135
K.D. Sethna's study	140
Supermind and the Omega Point	142
G. Mourge's study	144
10. JEAN GEBSER AND THE INVISIBLE ORIGIN	146
The Invisible Origin	147
Asia Smiles Differently	157
11. WHITEHEAD AND THE PROCESS PHILOSOPHY	161
Leibniz and the Monadology	162
Whitehead's philosophy	163

    The comparison – S.K. Maitra   168
    S.P. Singh's study   173
    Rod Hemsell's lectures   175
12. MODERN THEORIES OF EVOLUTION   177
13. SRI AUROBINDO'S ESSAY *EVOLUTION*   182

Literature   189
Index   191

Preface

Sri Aurobindo was a very creative and versatile author, his Complete Works comprise 36 volumes. During his stay in England he studied intensively the European cultural history and learnt several languages of the continent. He was primarily interested in poetry but also acquired some basic knowledge of Western philosophy, especially that of ancient Greece.

However, abstract thinking as such had little attraction for him and therefore he never read the works of Kant, Hegel, etc. But he was familiar with many philosophers and their basic thought and sometimes refers to them in his writings or talks. In some cases, these statements facilitate comparative research, as they provide some clues to his own understanding, thus giving the comparison a good foundation. His respective utterances will be quoted, whenever available, and analyzed in the various contexts. The main purpose of this study is to show how closely Sri Aurobindo's thought is related to European philosophy, and that in a certain way he even carried it on by taking up some basic approaches and deepening them in the light of a larger vision.

Our perspective is primarily that of Sri Aurobindo but we also try to do justice to all other philosophies discussed in this book. We hope that our research may inspire and facilitate further studies by presenting numberless relevant quotations which are interpreted in connection with kindred texts of Western thinkers, and by referring to some important books and articles dealing with the respective subjects. The references to Sri Aurobindo's titles are always to the Complete Works of Sri Aurobindo (CWSA), if not otherwise mentioned in the footnotes.

Our thanks are due to all those who made valuable suggestions for the improvement of the text or helped with the proof reading and editing.

Wilfried Huchzermeyer

Sri Aurobindo

1

The Life Divine

Sri Aurobindo had been a poet since his early youth; even at school he composed verses in several languages. The title of his philosophical main work too has a poetic sound due to the postpositioning of the adjective: The Life Divine. The book comprises about 1,000 pages, the greatest part of which was originally published in the journal *Arya* during the period 1914-1919. At a later stage Sri Aurobindo revised the text and added some chapters before it was published as a book in two parts in 1939-1940.

Sri Aurobindo's active interest in yoga had started in 1904 when he began practicing pranayama several hours a day. In 1908 he met the yogi Lele from Maharashtra and achieved an absolute silence of the mind after meditating with him for three days. After that he was no more "a labourer in a thought factory", as he once wrote in a letter, "but a receiver of knowledge from all the hundred realms of being".[1] He merely had to concentrate, and then the texts came to his mind in a steady flow of inspiration. However, the plane of inspiration was not always the same, therefore he later revised some texts so that they would express the new level which he had reached in the course of his spiritual path. This he also did with *The Life Divine* and especially with his epic poem *Savitri*.

Sri Aurobindo's philosophy

Sri Aurobindo's philosophy was developed in the tradition of Veda and Vedanta, as becomes obvious from the numerous quotations from the Rig Veda, the Upanishads and Bhagavadgita preceding the respective chapters. But it must be clarified that he gave his own specific interpretation to these ancient writings, establishing a close relation-

---

[1] *Letters on Himself and the Ashram*, 244

ship to his own thought. This applies especially to the Rig Veda which he considered a scripture with deep spiritual content, presenting in metaphorical language a holistic, world-affirming vision of the world. He has published his findings in *The Secret of the Veda* as well as some other writings.

According to Sri Aurobindo's vision, this world and the whole universe is a self-revelation of the Brahman, and whatever unfolds in evolution is already involved as a seed through involution.[2] There is the pure Spirit at the base of all Being, revealing itself with ever increasing degrees of consciousness, from matter to plant and animal to humans, whom however Sri Aurobindo does not consider the summit of creation. Higher stages of evolution will follow along with beings who will be able to manifest the Divine more perfectly than humans, even on the physical plane. In this regard Sri Aurobindo goes beyond the framework of Indian tradition, presenting a spiritual philosophy of evolution as has never been conceived before. Possibly, some Western influences are active here, as for instance impulses from Darwin or Nietzsche. But they always remain impulses or suggestions which he draws up in a transformed form to his own level of inspiration. He mentions Nietzsche's superman in two quotations in *The Life Divine* and, in greater detail, in a few other writings. From his viewpoint the German philosopher had some brilliant intuitions, but lacked that clarity of thinking which would have enabled him to differentiate between the asuric, anti-divine master-man and the spiritual, egoless humans of the future.

Darwin is also referred to in two passages. In the first Sri Aurobindo states that in respect to our possible higher evolution we are "much in the position of the original Ape of the Darwinian theory. It would have been impossible for that Ape leading his instinctive arboreal life in primeval forests to conceive that there would be one day an animal on the earth who would use a new faculty called reason upon the materials of his inner and outer existence."[3] This thought is significant and typical of Sri Aurobindo's philosophy. While our futurologists mostly follow a line of thinking which proceeds in a linear ascent

---

[2] This is only a simplified statement. Actually there are complex processes behind it, which will be presented in greater detail in some of the following chapters.
[3] *The Life Divine*, 60

from the present level without really leaving it, and enthrall our minds by imagining all kinds of future fabulous technical gadgetry, Sri Aurobindo dares to leap to another, still unknown plane, and enquires: "What will be next after *mind*?" His answer is *supermind*. This term plays an important role in *The Life Divine* and will therefore be expounded in the following text.

Supermind

Mind represents that level of evolution which is essentially characteristic of humans. It can produce a Plato, Kant or Shakespeare, but has its limits nonetheless. From Sri Aurobindo's viewpoint, mind is only capable of a fragmentary vision of things, it sees no more than parts of the Whole, never the Whole as such. But there are planes above the mind, the so-called *overhead* planes, which are capable of receiving a higher light. They are, in an ascending order, the higher, the illumined and the intuitive mind, and finally the overmind and supermind. A philosopher receiving illumined thoughts, a physicist making a great discovery through intuition, or a poet writing highly inspired verses – all of them go beyond the mind proper and receive something from hidden planes beyond it.

Overmind is, in Sri Aurobindo's terminology, the highest stage before supermind. It is a subordinate level of the supreme light, supporting the actual human evolution from Ignorance and building a bridge towards the highest Knowledge, which he also calls "Gnosis". Overmind receives the light of supermind, but divides it into separate aspects and forces. It is the world of the Gods.

Sri Aurobindo was convinced that the ancient Vedic Rishis had at least a partial realization of supermind, but they were not able to establish it on earth as a new evolutionary principle, as had happened at a certain stage with the principle of mind. But this exactly became his personal aim: as a pioneer progressing on the path of consciousness, he wanted to pave the way for others who would follow after him, facing less difficulties than the first forerunner. In his perception supermind is the dynamic truth-consciousness, the infinite wisdom and will of the Creator. It is that level through which the supreme Absolute, Sat-Chit-Ananda or Existence-Consciousness-Bliss, organizes

Creation; it is an intermediate power between the two spheres of the Infinite and the Finite, extending to both of them. He also calls it the "Real Idea", which is inherent in all cosmic existence, establishing the relationship to the world of becoming, the manifestation, and directing it. Supermind is the highest unifying consciousness which reconciles the antinomy of spirit and matter: the latter is seen as spirit-stuff and eventually even the body and its cells will be suffused with the Light, becoming a flexible instrument that is no longer subject to age and disease.

The psychic being

A brief summary of the content of *The Life Divine* would not be complete without mentioning the aspect of the heart plane and love. We find this treated in one of the last chapters, titled "The Triple Transformation". Sri Aurobindo explains here the psychic, spiritual and supramental transformation and expounds another special term of his yogic system, the psychic being. It is the soul *in evolution* through which contact with the Divine is being established. While the Atman is the immutable, immortal Self beyond birth and death, the psychic being could be described as a delegate of the Atman in the world of becoming. It develops progressively from life to life and has an increasing influence on the thinking, feeling and acting of the individual until the whole being is ready for the process of integral unification with the Divine.

The psychic impulse works primarily through the emotions turned towards the Divine, "through a love and adoration of the All-Beautiful and All-Blissful, the All-Good, the True."[4] This particular path of Bhakti can find its true fulfillment only in connection with a personal Divine. In *the Synthesis of Yoga* Sri Aurobindo points out: "... to approach God by love is to prepare oneself for the greatest possible spiritual fulfilment."[5]

---

[4] *The Life Divine*, 936
[5] *The Synthesis of Yoga*, 547

Heraclitus

2

Heraclitus – Being and Becoming

Nor is any Greek thinker more directly stimulating than the aphoristic philosopher Heraclitus, and yet he keeps and adds to this more modern intellectual stimulativeness something of the antique psychic and intuitive vision and word of the older Mystics.[1]

Heraclitus' account of the cosmos is an evolution and involution out of his one eternal principle of Fire.[2]

Sri Aurobindo

Sri Aurobindo's treatise on Heraclitus (ca. 535-475 B.C.) is the longest he ever wrote on a Western or Indian philosopher. His essay first appeared in 1916/17 in the journal *Arya* and was occasioned by a writing of the philosopher and Indologist Prof. R.D. Ranade in Pune, to which he refers repeatedly. There are also some prominent European thinkers of the past three centuries who composed lengthy commentaries on the famous Presocratic[3], including Hegel, Nietzsche and Heidegger. In ancient times, it was especially Plato and Aristotle who integrated some elements of his thought in their systems. Actually, we only know Heraclitus' writings from quotations of ancient authors; his work *On Nature*, completed at the beginning of the 5th century, was lost.

But what has induced Sri Aurobindo to dedicate a treatise of some forty pages to a philosopher who lived two and a half millennia ago? We find the answer right away in the first paragraph of his essay: he values the Greek philosophy as intellectually highly stimulating and full of significant knowledge. This is especially true of Heraclitus,

---

[1] *Essays in Philosophy and Yoga*, Heraclitus, 215
[2] Ibid., 233
[3] The term refers to philosophers before Socrates (469-399 B.C.).

who adds to it "something of the antique psychic and intuitive vision and word of the older Mystics." At least he was an intellectual child of the mystics, "although perhaps a rebel son in the house of his mother."[4] Sri Aurobindo sees Heraclitus, as the Upanishads, representing a period of transition when there was still a living inner vision, while at the same time a rational form of expression started establishing itself. This latter, he points out, fully unfolded itself a little later with the Sophists.

In ancient times, Heraclitus was called "the Obscure", because his aphorisms are somewhat inaccessible to the human mind, which resulted in the most divergent interpretations until the present age. However, for Sri Aurobindo his texts reflect the insights of a seer of a past age, expressing perceptions as are also found in the Vedic philosophy. Accordingly, he interprets some of Heraclitus' aphorisms against the background of kindred Vedic writings and their symbolism. In the following, we will present some examples showing the affinity of the two worlds.

Thunderbolt and fire

> This universe, the same for all beings, has not been created by any god or man, but it has always been, is and shall be an ever-living fire, regularly becoming ignited and regularly becoming extinguished. [30][5]
>
> It is the thunderbolt that steers the course of all things, *that is to say it directs it. For [Heraclitus] understands the thunderbolt to be the eternal fire. He also says that this fire is endowed with reason and cause of the whole world government.* [64]
>
> Immortals mortal, mortals immortal; the one living the other's death and dying the other's life. [62]

The ever-living fire, the thunderbolt steering all things, the Gods who are mortal, and humans who are immortal – these are indeed images we come across in the Rig Veda. Sri Aurobindo had studied this text

---

[4] Ibid., 215-16
[5] Heraclitus, *Aphorisms*. The translation follows mostly H. Diels' German text. The text in italics is that of the Greek commentator quoting Heraclitus.

intensively, revealing the key to its deep spiritual and psychological symbolism in his writing *The Secret of the Veda*.

Fire, Will, Force is, in the Vedic language, Agni, "the lord of the brilliant flame". He is "possessed of the Truth", "in mortals immortal", he "creates the gods".[6] Furthermore, we read: "These are thy flaming rays, O Strength, that go blazing violently and are like lightnings that run over all the quarters and are like a resonant chariot that speeds towards the plenitude." "The Will [Agni] is that which shines out in the gods, the Will is that which enters with its light into mortals." "This Flame shines out with the vast Light of the Truth and makes all things manifest by its greatness."[7]

In the Upanishads too we find some similar images. The Katha Upanishad 2.2.9-11 speaks of a Fire that has entered the world, shaping itself in many forms. It describes the Sun as the eye of this world, unstained from what it sees. One of the most beautiful similes is found in the Prashna Upanishad 1.8: "Fire is this burning, brilliant Sun. He[8] is the one Radiance and the all-knowing Light, he is the supreme heaven of the Spirit. He is shining with a thousand rays and exists in a hundred forms of being; behold, this rising Sun, He is the life of all His creatures."

We find the image of the thunderbolt in the Mahanarayana Upanishad 1.8, where it says that all the elements of Time, that is to say minutes, hours, seconds, arose from the thunderbolt, the Purusha. And further, we read in the Brihadaranyaka Upanishad 5.7.1 that "the Brahman is the thunderbolt." M.L. West, an English commentator on Heraclitus' aphorisms, writes with reference to the latter's use of the same image that the thunderbolt is exactly what was needed to combine the rival concepts of Zeus and a world fire. The thunderbolt is the traditional instrument of Zeus' will, "it distinguishes itself from ordinary fire by its ferocious power, its driving purposefulness."[9] At the end of his comparative study on Heraclitus and the Indian religion, West concludes "that the Brihadaranyaka Upanishad alone throws more light on what Heraclitus was talking about than all the remnants

---

[6] RV I.77.1. All the quotations from the Rig Veda are given in Sri Aurobindo's translation.
[7] RV V.10.5; V.25.4; V.2.9
[8] Sun, *surya*, is masculine in Sanskrit.
[9] *Early Greek Philosophy and the Orient*, Oxford 1971, p. 143

of the other Presocratics together."[10]

As already indicated, there are also some significant images in the Rig Veda that are closely related to aphorism 62: Immortals in mortals, mortals immortal. In this ancient text, it is a frequently used image that the godhead is called down into humans. Thus it says in RV V.82.7: "The universal godhead and master of being we accept into ourselves by perfect words today…"

Sri Aurobindo's commentary

In Sri Aurobindo's perception Heraclitus was great as a synthetic thinker reconciling opposites in an integral vision, especially Being and Becoming. Fire symbolizes both of them, having the aspect of permanence by constantly shining in the shape of the sun, but also the aspect of incessant becoming, by devouring and transforming objects with its flames. However, Heraclitus, in speaking of the ever living fire, "has clearly an idea of something more than a physical substance or energy":

> Fire is to him the physical aspect, as it were, of a great burning creative, formative and destructive force, the sum of all whose processes is a constant and unceasing change. The idea of the One which is eternally becoming Many and the Many which is eternally becoming One… is the foundation of Heraclitus' philosophy.[11]

The One, Sri Aurobindo points out, is not so much seen here as a stable substance, but rather as an active force, "a sort of substantial Will-to-become". But while for Nietzsche this latter will was all and everything, Heraclitus does not exclude Being as such from his view of things. He rather accepts both aspects of the ever flaming fire as simultaneously true: "Being is an eternal becoming and yet the Becoming resolves itself into eternal being. All is in flux, for all is change of becoming; we cannot step into the same waters twice, for it is other and yet other waters that are flowing on."[12] And yet it is one and the

---

[10] Ibid., 201
[11] *Essays in Philosophy and Yoga*, Heraclitus, 224
[12] Ibid.

same river as such.

Another well-known idea of the Greek thinker is that of war or strife as the father of all,[13] which describes the phenomenon of a clash of forces, bringing about, through competition, creative progress. And thirdly, there is the idea of an evolutionary movement upwards and downwards, called in Indian philosophy *pravṛtti* and *nivṛtti*, the process of emerging and manifesting and of ceasing and dissolving. "These are the master ideas of the thought of Heraclitus."[14]

The idea of evolution

The way up and down is one and the same.[15]

In chapter 4 of his essay on Heraclitus Sri Aurobindo interprets the above-mentioned aphorism and points out: "Heraclitus' account of the cosmos is an evolution and involution out of his one eternal principle of Fire, – at once the one substance and the one force, – which he expresses in his figurative language as the upward and downward road."[16] Out of Fire, Sri Aurobindo continues, air, water and earth proceed, which is "the procession of energy on its downward road." But there is equally immanent in it a force of potential return, "which would lead things backward to their source in the reverse order." The whole cosmic action is based on this balanced play of forces of contrary energies:

The movement of life is like the back-returning of the bow, to which [Heraclitus] compares it, an energy of traction and tension restraining an energy of release, every force of action compensated by a corresponding force of reaction. By the resistance of one to the other all the harmonies of existence are created.[17]

Next Sri Aurobindo refers, by way of comparison, to the ancient Indi-

---

[13] Fragment 53.
[14] *Essays in Philosophy and Yoga,* Heraclitus, 225
[15] Heraclitus, fragment 60.
[16] *Essays in Philosophy and Yoga,* Heraclitus, 233
[17] Ibid.

an Sankhya philosophy which had developed a similar idea of a successive evolution of conditions of energy out of a first substance, *pradhāna*, from which evolve the 24 so-called Tattvas or basic categories, in the physical world ether, air, fire, water and earth. However, this is not our subject here, we only have to note the essential difference between the Greek and Indian systems of philosophy, described by Sri Aurobindo as follows:

> But the Greeks failed to go forward to that final discrimination... - [on the one hand] the discrimination between Prakriti and her cosmic principles, her twenty-four tattwas forming the subjective and objective aspects of Nature, and [on the other hand] between Prakriti and Purusha, Conscious-Soul and Nature-Energy.[18]

Thus, the early Greeks were not able to arrive at the idea of pure energy and "the fire of Heraclitus has to do duty at once for the original substance of all Matter and for God and Eternity."

> This preoccupation with Nature-Energy and the failure to fathom its relations with Soul has persisted in modern scientific thought, and we find there too the same attempt to identify some primary principle of Nature, ether or electricity, with the original Force.[19]

Nevertheless, there remains the fact of a common approach in the theory of creation, that is to say the idea of evolutionary change out of the original substance. Sri Aurobindo next refers once more to the "upward and downward road", discussing the above-mentioned Indian concept of *pravṛtti* and *nivṛtti*, the process of moving out and forward and of moving back and inward. It meant on the one hand the entering of the soul into manifestation and withdrawal from it; and on the other hand, also the periodical becoming and dissolving of creation, the latter being called *pralaya*. Sri Aurobindo thinks that Heraclitus may have had something similar in mind and refers to a fragment[20] of the

---

[18] Ibid., 234
[19] Ibid.
[20] In Greek philosophy, the term refers to short, incomplete extracts from original texts, quoted by other philosophers or commentators.

Stoics which supports this thesis by stating that Heraclitus believed in the theory of conflagration, "an assertion which they are hardly likely to have made if this were not generally accepted as his teaching."[21]

Next he proceeds to interpret Fragment 10, "out of all the One and out of One all":

> Heraclitus' affirmation is not simply that the One is always Many, the Many always One, but ... it means a constant current and back-current of change, the upward and downward road, and we may suppose that as the One by downward change becomes completely the All in the descending process, yet remains eternally the one everliving Fire, so the All by upward change may resort completely to the One and yet essentially exist, since it can again return into various being by the repetition of the downward movement. All difficulty [in accepting the theory of conflagration] disappears if we remember that what is implied is a process of evolution and involution, – so too the Indian word for creation, *sṛṣṭi*, means a release or bringing forth of what is held in, latent, – and that the conflagration destroys existing forms, but not the principle of multiplicity. There will be then no inconsistency at all in Heraclitus' theory of a periodic conflagration; it is rather, that being the highest expression of change, the complete logic of his system.[22]

Furthermore, Sri Aurobindo points out with reference to the Isha Upanishad that the latter too describes the cosmos as universal motion and becoming. The Sanskrit word *jagat*, world, contains the root *gam*, to go, to move. Accordingly, the macrocosm "is one vast principle of motion and therefore of change and instability, while each thing in the universe is in itself a microcosm of the same motion and instability."[23]

The relation between God and World, Sri Aurobindo continues, is summed up in the phrase, "It is He that has moved out everywhere." *He* is the Lord, the Seer and thinker, corresponding to Heraclitus' Logos, his Zeus, the One out of which arise all things. *He* has fixed all things according to their nature from years sempiternal, which again corresponds to Heraclitus' statement "All things are fixed and deter-

---

[21] Ibid., 235
[22] *Essays in Philosophy and Yoga*, Heraclitus, 235f
[23] Ibid., 228

mined". Sri Aurobindo arrives at the following conclusion:

> Substitute [Heraclitus'] Fire for the Vedantic Atman and there is nothing in the expressions of the Upanishad which the Greek thinker would not have accepted as another figure of his own thought. And do not the Upanishads use among other images this very symbol of the Fire? "As one Fire has entered into the world and taken shapes according to the various forms in the world," so the one Being has become all these names and forms and yet remains the One.[24]

The Logos

Sri Aurobindo has explained in his philosophical main work *The Life Divine* that there is, from his viewpoint, a plan behind evolution which gives it a certain direction. In this context, we may enquire now whether in Heraclitus' philosophy too there is a kind of hidden law behind the permanent becoming and dissolving. Here the Greek term Logos comes in. It originally means word, language, thought, but with Heraclitus stands for a universal law or reason which remains inaccessible for "the many", revealing itself only to those who make an intensive effort to fathom it. In his longest aphorism, Fragment 1, he points out:

> But this Logos, though eternal, humans are not able to understand, neither before hearing it nor after having first heard it. For even though all things come to pass in accordance with this Logos, humans seem not to understand them, when they make trial of words and deeds such as I set forth, analyzing each thing according to its nature and indicating how it truly is.

It is up to the few chosen people to realize the Logos and act according to it. In this context, Heraclitus comments in Fragment 112:

> Right consciousness[25] is the highest virtue, and wisdom is to speak

---

[24] Ibid, 228
[25] Greek *sophronein*, also translated as "self-control".

truth and consciously act according to nature.

We will examine now how Sri Aurobindo treats the subject of Logos in chapter 6 of his essay *Heraclitus*. The One, he points out, is to Heraclitus (as to the Vedanta philosophers) an absolute. Under its roof day and night, good and evil are united and free from the differentiations made in the relative world.

There is a Word, a Reason in all things, a Logos, and that Reason is one; only men by the relativeness of their mentality turn it each into his personal thought and way of looking at things and live according to this variable relativity. It follows that there is an absolute, a divine way of looking at things. "To God all things are good and just, but men hold some things to be good, others unjust."[26]

So there is an absolute Good, absolute Beauty and Justice of which all things are a relative expression. There is a divine order in this world and each thing fulfills its nature according to its place in this order, Sri Aurobindo continues. From a highest viewpoint, everything – Good as well as Evil – fulfills itself according to a divine purpose. However, this is not to say that the relative viewpoint would be without validity. Rather it is naturally taken by humans, and Heraclitus states in Fragment 114: "Fed are all human laws by one, the divine."[27] Sri Aurobindo concludes that "Heraclitus admits relative standards, but as a thinker he is obliged to go beyond them."[28]

In another passage in the 7th chapter Sri Aurobindo once more refers to the meaning of Logos and says that it is "an intelligent Force which is the origin and master of things... The Logos is one and universal, an absolute reason therefore combining and managing all the relativities of the many."[29] Next Sri Aurobindo mentions the "seed Logos" of the Stoics, *spermatikos*, "reproduced in conscious beings as a number of seed Logoi,"[30] and refers to similar ideas in the Vedanta.

---

[26] *Essays in Philosophy and Yoga*, Heraclitus, 242. At the end of the text Sri Aurobindo translates Heraclitus' fragment no. 102.
[27] Sri Aurobindo's translation.
[28] *Essays in Philosophy and Yoga,* Heraclitus, 243
[29] Ibid., 250
[30] Ibid., 251

These lead us to the important Sanskrit term Vijnana which he frequently uses as a synonym for *supermind* in works such as *The Synthesis of Yoga*.

> Vijnana is indeed a consciousness which sees things, not as the human reason sees them in parts and pieces, in separated and aggregated relations, but in the original reason of their existence and law of their existence, their primal and total truth; therefore it is the seed Logos, the originative and determinant conscious force working as supreme Intelligence and Will. The Vedic seers called it the Truth-consciousness and believed that men also could become truth-conscious, enter into the divine Reason and Will and by the Truth become immortals, *anthropoi athanatoi*.[31]

Criticism

Even while Sri Aurobindo praises in many ways Heraclitus' deep force of knowledge, he also points out a certain shortcoming which from his viewpoint is characteristic as well of the later European thinking:

> But his knowledge of the truth of things stopped with the vision of the universal reason and the universal force... The eye of the Indian thought saw a third aspect of the Self and of Brahman..., it saw the universal delight active in divine love and joy. European thought, following the line of Heraclitus' thinking, has fixed itself on reason and on force and made them the principles towards whose perfection our being has to aspire.[32]

According to Sri Aurobindo, Western thought only saw two lower aspects of this delight (Sanskrit *ananda*), that is to say pleasure and aesthetic beauty, whereas it missed spiritual beauty and delight. "For that reason Europe has never been able to develop a powerful religion of its own; it has been obliged to turn to Asia."[33]

---

[31] Ibid.
[32] Ibid., 252
[33] Ibid., 253

Nevertheless, Sri Aurobindo concedes that Heraclitus came very close to the secret of this third aspect by stating that "the kingdom is of the child", his "profoundest utterance".[34] "For this kingdom is evidently spiritual, it is the crown, the mastery to which the perfected man arrives; and the perfect man is a divine child! He is the soul which awakens to the divine play…"[35]

---

[34] Ibid., 252. The reference is to Fragment 52. In the first part it says, "Eternity is a child playing draughts."
[35] Ibid., 253

Plato

3

Plato – The Theory of Ideas

Why should the stream[1] be, as Heraclitus himself admits, the same stream although it is ever other and other waters that are flowing? It was in this connection that Plato brought in his eternal, ideal plane of fixed ideas, by which he seems to have meant at once an originating real-idea and an original ideal schema for all things.[2]

But even without religion philosophy by itself can give us at least some light on the spiritual destiny of man, some hope of the infinite, some ideal perfection after which we can strive. Plato who was influenced by Heraclitus, tried to do this for us; his thought sought after God, tried to seize the ideal, had its hope of a perfect human society.[3]

Plato was a great writer as well as a philosopher – no more perfect prose has been written by any man.[4]

Sri Aurobindo

Along with Socrates and Aristotle the philosopher Plato[5] (427-347) is one of the greatest thinkers of ancient Greece. He became well-known especially through his theory of ideas and his state philosophy. Nearly all of his prose writings are composed as dialogues, and it is almost always his teacher Socrates who is in the centre of these talks, which seek to achieve knowledge through the art of deep questioning. Plato has not created any particular scheme of philosophy, but we may extract from his many writings a kind of doctrine. However, we have to note that his views were not always constant; they could change in

---

[1] Sri Aurobindo refers here to the stream as such, as a form or idea.
[2] *Essays in Philosophy and Yoga*, Heraclitus, 238
[3] Ibid., 248
[4] *Letters on Poetry and Art*, 522
[5] "Plato" is the Latin version, in Greek it is "Platon".

some respects and undergo some development. There are hints in his letters which suggest that possibly he further dwelt on a few ideas mentioned in the dialogues, without committing them to paper. Until the present time scholars often vary in their interpretations of his thoughts, but nonetheless a few essential points can be considered as ascertained. It is certain too that Plato's philosophy has had a unique influence on European cultural history up to the present day.

Sri Aurobindo had studied Plato's works *Symposium* and *Republic* in the original Greek language as a student in England, and mentions them as great literary works in *The Life Divine*. Plato conceived the ideal of a perfect society and tried to realize it at the court of Dionysius II in Syracuse, but failed completely. In contrast, Sri Aurobindo engaged himself in the Indian independence movement and was able to give it some important impulses. Later on, after having moved to Pondicherry to develop his path of integral yoga, he wrote his title *The Ideal of Human Unity* in which he presented his vision of a progressive future development of human society.

Plato's theory of ideas

The theory of ideas is Plato's most well-known contribution to European philosophy and also the best starting point for a comparison with the thought of Sri Aurobindo, as the latter had developed the term Real-Idea in connection with his concept of supermind. But we will first examine Plato's thoughts. The term "idea" in his works has a special meaning: the ideas are the archetypes behind all that is, they are the true Being, whereas the objects perceptible to the senses only have a conditioned, secondary, derived existence.

The ideas are perfect, not accessible to sense perception; they can only be perceived by reason. They are beyond time and neither become nor dissolve nor undergo any change. They are also beyond space and formless, but cause spatial forms.

The idea embodies its content, such as Goodness, in its purest form, without any shadow of contrariness. It is self-existent, whereas its images or reflections are dependent on it and fed by it. While the images form the world of multiplicity, the idea stands for the unity behind all things.

The ideas are interconnected and can be envisioned in the shape of a hierarchical structure. The more general and comprehensive idea has always a superior status and at the top there is "the Good", to which are subordinated the categories of the existent, the movement, stasis as well as the identical and the different. The ideas are like divine beings who are even higher ranked than the Gods. Actually, the latter have divinity because of their access to the ideas.

The phenomena of the physical world are reflections of the ideas, with different degrees of participation (*metexis*) in them. The ideas, by extending as it were into the physical world, convey values such as beauty, goodness or justice.

Sri Aurobindo's Real-Idea

Having presented Plato's basic thoughts, we will next examine Sri Aurobindo's concept of Real-Idea, as introduced by him in *The Life Divine*. In chapter I, 13, titled The Divine Maya, he points out that noumenalistic philosophers posit the principle of mind, thought, idea as Creator, but this absolute does not have any actual relation to the relative world. The philosophy of idealism, he continues, goes a step further by establishing a relation between the truth behind the phenomenon and the phenomenon as such. Finally, he explains his own position:

> The view I am presenting goes farther in idealism; it sees the creative Idea as Real-Idea, that is to say, a power of Conscious-Force expressive of real being, born out of real being and partaking of its nature and neither a child of the Void nor a weaver of fictions. It is conscious Reality throwing itself into mutable forms of its own imperishable and immutable substance. The world is therefore not a figment of conception in the universal Mind, but a conscious birth of that which is beyond Mind into forms of itself.[6]

In the next chapter, The Supermind as Creator, Sri Aurobindo specifically discusses the difference between the mental consciousness and

---

[6] *The Life Divine*, 125

the truth consciousness. In the first, thought is regarded as something separate, "abstract, unsubstantial, different from reality", something that detaches itself from the objective reality in order to observe, understand and judge. But in supermind this division does not exist, here being and consciousness are one, and the idea is "an initial coming out, in creative self-knowledge, of that which lay concentrated in uncreative self-awareness":

> It comes out as Idea that is a reality, and it is that reality of the Idea which evolves itself, always by its own power and consciousness of itself, always self-conscious, always self-developing by the will inherent in the idea, always self-realising by the knowledge ingrained in its every impulsion. This is the truth of all creation, of all evolution.[7]

In another passage, Sri Aurobindo even arrives at a direct equation of Real-Idea and Supermind:

> But then it appears immediately that as Mind is only a final operation of Supermind, so Life is only a final operation of the Consciousness-Force of which Real-Idea is the determinative form and creative agent. Consciousness that is Force is the nature of Being and this conscious Being manifested as creative Knowledge-Will is the Real-Idea or Supermind.[8]

It is a common experience in ordinary human life that we receive a multitude of ideas, but only some of them are successfully worked out in actuality. In contrast, Sri Aurobindo sees the Real-Idea endowed with an inherent force of self-fulfilment in the relative world of becoming, on all the planes of mind, life and matter. In humans we find this occurrence reflected in the form of a will inspired by supreme knowledge and therefore seeking and undertaking precisely those actions which can be actually realized – it is "a will that is eventually self-effective because it is of the substance of Knowledge and a faith that is the reflex in the lower consciousness of a Truth or real Idea yet

---

[7] Ibid., 138
[8] Ibid., 201

unrealised in the manifestation."⁹

Sri Aurobindo thus refers to a stage of consciousness which according to his vision awaits humans in future evolution, enabling them to act in accordance with the highest truth and thereby giving creation a new shape and quality. By acting out of a unified consciousness, humans would overcome the patterns of behaviour based on mutual opposition and hostility, replacing them by creative cooperation – a vision applying not only to the life of individuals in a community, but also to the life of nations and their international relations.

The differences

We may enquire now how far the two concepts of Plato's Idea and Sri Aurobindo's Real-Idea concur or diverge. In the quotation printed at the beginning of this chapter, Sri Aurobindo himself reveals a connection by stating that Plato seems to have meant with his eternal, ideal plane of fixed ideas at once an originating real-idea and an original ideal schema for all things. However, the predicate "seems" in Sri Aurobindo's commentary shows that he was not altogether sure about this interpretation.¹⁰

The Indian professor of philosophy S.K. Maitra investigates the two concepts critically in his standard work *The Meeting of the East and the West in Sri Aurobindo's Philosophy*¹¹ and analyses especially the differences. From his viewpoint, one of the major defects of Plato's theory of ideas is his conceiving the ideas as static entities without creative force. Only the souls have this force in his system and therefore God, who is regarded as the highest soul, has the creative function. In other words, the ideas themselves cannot establish any direct connection with the world of senses, it only becomes possible through God as mediator, playing a secondary role as it were as an executive

---

⁹ *The Synthesis of Yoga*, 44
¹⁰ See also A.B. Purani, *Evening Talks with Sri Aurobindo* (2007), pp. 496f: In a talk dated 24-8-1926 a disciple says, he believes Plato did not mean a mental abstraction by his *ideas*, but rather a "creative conception". Sri Aurobindo replies that Plato had "very mathematical ideas about these things". In case he had a creative conception, it may have included the Real Idea. A little later Sri Aurobindo adds: "I do not know if Plato had some dim intimation of the Supramental; but as his mind was mathematical he cast it into rigid rational and mental forms. That was the Greek mind."
¹¹ Pondicherry, Sri Aurobindo Ashram 1968.

agent of the ideas. As for the human world, God does not create it directly, but leaves it to inferior powers, according to Plato. Maitra resumes: "This gives the human world a much lower status than what it would have if it had direct connection with the ideas. Although it is supposed to participate in the ideas, such participation can only be very imperfect."[12]

Maitra sees another significant difference in Plato's system as compared to Sri Aurobindo's: Plato did not develop any evolutionary theory. Individuals may be able through education to achieve a vision of the highest ideas such as the Good and make some personal progress through it, but there is no goal or destiny towards which the world as a whole would move.

On the other hand, for Sri Aurobindo evolution is a crucial element of his philosophy. Through involution the Spirit is imbedded in creation on all levels and seeks to rediscover itself through evolution. This gradual process of awakening brings about in the long run a realisation of the Good, True and Beautiful not only in the individual, but also in the society and in nations. In this context we may speak of an evolutionary optimism which is characteristic of Sri Aurobindo's vision.

However, in spite of these differences Maitra recognizes that Plato had remarkable intuitions helping him to acquire some deep knowledge. In Maitra's analysis, his problem was that mental elements in the form of logic and reason came in, causing a conflict between the latter and the intuition, and Plato was not able to create a true synthesis, as Sri Aurobindo did by determining for all planes their respective roles, limits and possibilities.

K.D. Sethna's analysis

K.D. Sethna discusses this same topic in his title *Sri Aurobindo and Greece*[13], presenting a commentary which is less critical than Maitra's and rather emphasises common features in the two philosophies. His starting point is the above mentioned first quotation at the beginning

---

[12] *Maitra*, 216
[13] Pondicherry, 1998

of this chapter, complemented by further passages from *The Life Divine*, some of which have already been quoted in the present chapter. Sethna explains the connection of the mental, vital and physical planes with the higher planes with the help of the following statement of Sri Aurobindo:

> Mind, Life and Body are an inferior consciousness and a partial expression which strives to arrive in the mould of a various evolution at that superior expression of itself already existent to the Beyond-Mind. That which is in the Beyond-Mind is the ideal which in its own conditions it is labouring to realise.[14]

The term Beyond-Mind here refers generally to all planes beyond mind proper. But there is also the term overmind which denotes a specific higher plane. As supermind is the link between the highest Absolute and the world of relative appearances, overmind is a link between supermind and the world of ignorance. In overmind the highest truth consciousness works with a reduced force and integrality: "The one total and many-sided Real-Idea is split up into its many sides; each becomes an independent Idea-Force with the power to realise itself," declares Sri Aurobindo.[15]

Now it is K.D. Sethna's impression that Plato was often uncertain and wavering in his knowledge, because he had no access to the highest plane of vision, that is to say the supramental: "Many of his ambiguities appear to stem from his mind's translation of the Overmind's version, rather than the Supermind's authenticity, of the Real-Idea."[16] Sethna then presents a quotation from Plato which a disciple once sent Sri Aurobindo along with a question. Plato's statement runs as follows:

> The world of sense is the copy of the world of Ideas. In our visible world there is a graduation of beings... The same holds true of the intelligible realm or pattern of the world; the Ideas are joined together by means of other Ideas of a higher order; ... the Ideas constantly in-

---

[14] *The Life Divine*, 125-26
[15] *The Life Divine*, 295
[16] *Sri Aurobindo and Greece*, 75

crease in generality and force, until we reach the top, the last, the highest, the most powerful Idea or the Good, which comprehends, contains or summarizes the entire system.

With reference to this quotation, Sri Aurobindo was asked the following question: is Plato here not on the verge of understanding in mind the realization of the overmind? Or can the passage be interpreted as being due merely to mental ideas? Sri Aurobindo answered:

> [Plato] was trying to express in a mental way the One containing the multiplicity which is brought out (created) from the One, - that is the Overmind realisation. Plato has these ideas not as realisations but as intuitions which he expressed in his own mental form.[17]

So Sri Aurobindo holds that Plato had indeed a kind of understanding of the plane of overmind, but he has only "tapped" it as it were, receiving something from it per intuition. However, these intuitions are not of the same nature as realisations, for the latter are the specific achievements of mystics or yogis, whereas Plato is, from Sri Aurobindo's viewpoint, a great inspired thinker. A realisation implies the permanent assimilation of a spiritual experience, with a distinct effect not only on thinking but also on life. In this context, K.D. Sethna quotes Sri Aurobindo: "One would never think of applying such a term [mystic] to Spinoza, Kant or Hegel: even Plato does not fit into the term, though Pythagoras has a good claim to it. Hegel and other transcendental or idealistic philosophers were great intellects, not mystics."[18] Nonetheless, Plato occupies a very special, elevated position due to his intuitive vision, which Sri Aurobindo misses in Aristotle whom he found very "dry" and "mental".

Sethna next shows in a very perceptive analysis how Sri Aurobindo has overcome the weak points in Plato's system:

> Some of the ambiguities of the Platonic intuition arise from lack of knowledge of the "various evolution" that Sri Aurobindo speaks of.

---

[17] *Letters on Poetry and Art*, 519
[18] *Sri Aurobindo and Greece*, 71

Evolution implies in the Aurobindonian scheme the hidden activity of real-ideas within the phenomenal flux, their godhead lying in a state of "involution" and gradually awaking to their own glorious plenitude until what is flawless above is manifested in a flawlessness below. That complete self-disclosure of the Divine on earth in a radiant future was utterly beyond Plato's conception, however much he might dream of a political Utopia. Dim approximation, temporary *à peu près* – this constituted in his philosophy all that was possible of the True, the Beautiful and the Good in the kingdom of man.[19]

In spite of this difference we may sum up that there was hardly any other Western thinker in ancient times who came so close to Sri Aurobindo's concept of supermind as Plato with his theory of ideas. Conversely, Sri Aurobindo with his new interpretation of Plato has thrown new light on his insights, possibly revealing through it their true and deepest meaning. As a follow-up to the above-mentioned correspondence on Plato's intuitions the disciple asked another interesting question: "There are many such thoughts in Plato's philosophy. Did he get them from Indian books?" Sri Aurobindo answered:

> Not from Indian books – something of the philosophy of India got through by means of Pythagoras and others. But I think Plato got most of these things from intuition.[20]

Finally, we have to mention that Plato – like Pythagoras – believed in an immortal soul and rebirth. However, these are subjects whose discussion would be in place in a general comparison with Indian philosophy rather than in a specific one with Sri Aurobindo, as with the latter there are hardly any particular points of reference. But noteworthy is in any case Plato's belief that the soul, before its entry into the human body, has seen the pure Ideas at a transcendental place and is now gradually remembering this fore-knowledge (anamnesis) in its earthly existence. Similarly, from Sri Aurobindo's viewpoint too all knowledge is already within us. Through Sadhana, spiritual discipline,

---

[19] *Sri Aurobindo and Greece*, 76
[20] *Letters on Poetry and Art*, 520

the soul is freed from its shackles on the integral yoga path and is therefore more and more able to emerge. Furthermore, on the level of consciousness there is an opening of the higher planes beyond Mind, accompanied by a descent of ever increasing knowledge.

Plotinus with some students

4

Plotinus and the *Nous*

Plotinus was not a mere philosopher, – his philosophy was founded on yogic experience and realisation.[1]

The ideas of the Upanishads can be rediscovered in much of the thought of Pythagoras and Plato and form the profoundest part of Neo-Platonism and Gnosticism with all their considerable consequences to the philosophical thinking of the West.[2]

Sri Aurobindo

The Neo-Platonic philosopher Plotinus (205-270 A.D.) is much less well-known than Plato, but Sri Aurobindo and some of his disciples were familiar with his name and thought. Plotinus created a highly developed philosophy of emanation centering around the Greek term *Nous*, which is to be pronounced as *Nūs* and might be rendered as spirit, world-spirit, intellect or intelligence. Teilhard de Chardin's term *Noosphere* has been derived from it, and English words such as *noetic* are related to it. There are some letters and talks of Sri Aurobindo in which he refers to this subject. In the following, we will at first present and analyze his various statements made in different contexts, before exploring Plotinus's philosophy as such.

In October 1933 he was corresponding on Plotinus with a disciple and made the appreciative remark given above in the first place. In the course of this correspondence the disciple quotes a short text of the philosopher in order to get Sri Aurobindo's opinion regarding its meaning. It is to be noted that in the quotation below the term *Nous* does not occur as such, but it is actually present in the word *intelligence*, which has been chosen here as its English equivalent:

---

[1] *Letters on Poetry and Art*, 522
[2] *The Renaissance in India*, 330

Intelligence is the first divine emanation... Creation is a fall, a progressive degeneration of the divine. In the intelligence, the absolute unity of God splits up into intelligence proper... and the intelligible world.[3]

After having presented this quotation, the disciple proceeds to ask Sri Aurobindo whether Plotinus might be referring to the plane of overmind here – that plane in which (in Sri Aurobindo's system) the pure unity of supermind is split up into separate aspects and forces.

Sri Aurobindo responds that Plotinus probably speaks of the "cosmic mind". The latter term is not very common in Sri Aurobindo's philosophy; it occurs a few times in *The Life Divine* and is closely related to *overmind*. It is a plane in which division and partition already exists, but with the memory of the original unity still active. There is a passage in which Sri Aurobindo explains that the cosmic mind is "in direct contact with the Supramental Truth-consciousness", it is...

an Overmind that covers as with the wide wings of some creative Oversoul this whole lower hemisphere of Knowledge-Ignorance, links it with that greater Truth-Consciousness while yet at the same time with its brilliant golden Lid it veils the face of the greater Truth from our sight...[4]

Subsequent to this commentary on Plotinus' text Sri Aurobindo points out that in these philosophies no distinction is made between different grades of mind or between intellect and the consciousness beyond the intellectual. Finally, after another question of the disciple he adds that Plotinus may have meant by "intelligence" that which is called *buddhi* in Sanskrit, "but endows the *buddhi* with the qualities proper to the Intuition and Overmind." These are significant statements, no doubt, but they are somewhat complicated and not easy to follow. However, we can note that Sri Aurobindo does see in the above quotation a con-

---

[3] Ibid., 522-523
[4] *The Life Divine*, 292

nection between the "intelligence" (which is actually *Nous*) and his overmind.

Sri Aurobindo was not aware of the Greek term at this stage, but seven years later he chanced upon it in his readings and asked his disciple Purani: "Do you know anything about the *Nous*, the Divine Mind, of Plotinus? Krishnaprem[5] appears to make the Supermind and the *Nous* the same. *Nous* seems to be Intelligence."[6] So we find Sri Aurobindo using here as a translation the term *divine Mind*, which he explains in *The Life Divine* as "a subordinate and not really a separate function of the Real-Idea, of the Supermind."[7] He compares it with the consciousness of a poet looking at his own creations, which for the purpose of the vision appear separate from him, even though they are and remain part of himself.

A few months later Purani presents to Sri Aurobindo a book on Plotinus by the English author Dean Inge.[8] After having looked at a few pages, Sri Aurobindo comments: "Inge takes *Nous* as Spirit. As far as I can make out, *Nous* is spiritual consciousness, not Supermind, but I will see about it again."[9] So after the cosmic and the divine mind a third term is given here, which Sri Aurobindo explains at another place as follows:

> The spiritual consciousness is that in which we enter into the awareness of Self, the Spirit, the Divine and are able to see in all things their essential reality and the play of forces and phenomena as proceeding from that essential Reality.[10]

In December 1940 Sri Aurobindo mentions Inge's book once more, without however giving his final view on the term *Nous*. His various statements show that the exact attribution of a term in comparative studies is often very difficult because there are different systems of thought behind the respective philosophies, with only a partial over-

---

[5] Ronald Nixon, an American spiritual author who greatly appreciated Sri Aurobindo's writings.
[6] Nirodbaran, *Talks with Sri Aurobindo*, 9 June 1940
[7] *The Life Divine*, 175
[8] William Ralph Inge, Dean of St. Paul's. His book is titled *The Philosophy of Plotinus,* London 1929.
[9] Nirodbaran, *Talks with Sri Aurobindo*, 23 October 1940
[10] SABCL 22:316

lapping of terms and their meaning. However, it has to be mentioned that Sri Aurobindo's designation of *Nous* as "Divine Mind" or "spiritual consciousness" cannot be regarded as absolutely certain, as the text was taken from the *Talks with Sri Aurobindo* and Nirodbaran himself has said that the records, based on his notes and memory, are faithful, but not necessarily exact literal renderings. Therefore, the greatest weight should be given to Sri Aurobindo's statements given in the letters.

We will try now to shed some more light on the question of similarities in the concepts of *Nous* and overmind or supermind and will begin with a brief look at the life and philosophy of Plotinus, who was the most important Neo-Platonic thinker of the 3rd century A.D.

Plotinus' life and philosophy

Plotinus grew up in Alexandria, Egypt, and had some contact there with a philosopher who introduced him to Plato's teachings. Later on he moved on to Rome where he founded a philosophical school. Until the end of his life he was a highly reputed person, which was also due to his noble and sincere conduct of life. For some time he had plans to study the local philosophy in Persia and India, but these plans failed due to certain political circumstances.

There are reports that he had some supernatural gifts, what is called "siddhis" in yoga literature. Thus he is said to have been able to recognize thieves at first sight and to be able to know intuitively the state of consciousness of humans whom he met, or even to have a foreknowledge of their future. His biographer Prophyrios reports that he experienced four times the highest ecstatic states, with visions of the supreme Divine beyond all forms.

But, as many mystics in the past, he had a strong aversion against his physical body – he even considered it a shame to dwell with his soul in a body and did not allow portraits to be made of his face. His birthday he kept secret as he did not believe it to be a great event to have become a human being. Plotinus' last words before his death have been reported to be: "Strive to give back the Divine in yourselves to the Divine in the All."[11]

In his philosophy Plotinus posits a divine Being which is One and All, infinite, indivisible beyond time and space, but basically ineffable and beyond the reach of human language. Here we feel reminded of the "speechlessness" of the Upanishadic seers who ultimately arrived at the statement, *neti, neti*, "it is not this, it is not that". But how is the world of multiplicity created? This is a difficult question for Plotinus, because from his viewpoint the One is perfect in itself, it does not seek anything, does not require anything, it is the absolute fullness.

He finds a kind of answer in the image of the overflowing of the fullness which creates something out of itself without becoming more or less in itself, comparable to the sun emitting its rays or to humans generating their image in a mirror. Here too we feel reminded of a mantra of the Upanishads, *oṁ pūrṇam adaḥ...*, "Fullness there, fullness here. From fullness flows fullness. Taking fullness from fullness away, fullness remains nonetheless fulfilled."[12]

According to Plotinus' system of emanation, *Nous*, the world-spirit, is the first element to arise from the Transcendent One. Johannes Hirschberger, author of a standard history of philosophy, describes *Nous* as follows: "It is the epitome of all ideas, norms, laws and structures of being, it is the kosmos noetos [the world of pure forms] and at the same time the platonic demiurge. It is still very close to the Primeval One, its image, the glimpse as it were with which the One looks at itself."[13] Similarly, Sri Aurobindo had used the image of "the poet looking at his own creations", when defining the divine Mind.

Thus *Nous* is the highest stage of the Existent; being and thinking are united in it, and we find the Beautiful and the Good in their purest form. On this plane "thought is not discursive deducting, but the direct grasping of that which is thought"[14] – a description similar to that of Sri Aurobindo's supermind, which is marked by its direct knowledge of Truth without the need of reasoning and inference. Furthermore it is said that *Nous* is an objective reality, a world of thought which exists independent of the individual beings. The individual that turns to-

---

[11] *The Six Enneads*, translated by S. MacKenna and B.S. Page.
[12] Brihadaryanka Upanishad 5.1.1
[13] *Geschichte der Philosophie*, Bd. 1, Freiburg 1980, p. 307
[14] German Wikipedia, „Plotin".

wards this realm, does not produce his own thoughts, but rather grasps its content by partaking in the world of the spirit. As pure Spirit, *Nous* is essentially one, but at the same time manifold because it contains a multiplicity of ideas.

At a further stage, the world-soul (*psyche*) emerges from the *Nous* and is then divided into individual souls. And finally, at the lowest stage, the material world of sense objects emerges from it. Matter as such is considered by Plotinus as not perceivable, "non-existent", although visible forms are created out of it through the soul. Thus, matter is as it were the most distant and most darkened horizon in the unfolding of the One which extends into multiplicity with different degrees of perfection, without losing its oneness.

This would be the description of one aspect of the world process, the way "downward" into multiplicity. But there is, from the perspective of the individual, also the way "upward", which involves detachment from the physical world, self-purification and connecting with the *Nous* and finally through it a re-unification with the Primeval One. At this point we understand what Sri Aurobindo meant when once he noted in the *Evening Talks*: "Plotinus takes up a position, in which the true world is not here but above."[15]

Thus we may resume: although Plotinus' *Nous* (in connection with what he calls "soul") as an epitome of all ideas and as creative world-organizing force does have some affinity with Sri Aurobindo's supermind, his philosophy totally lacks that positive vision of the world and evolution which is so distinctive of Sri Aurobindo's thought. Supermind is meant to bring the full force of the Spirit into life and matter for the sake of their fulfilment. There is a purpose in all manifestation, namely the joyful self-experience of the Divine through the progressive illumination of an initially unenlightened world.

By way of contrast, creation with Plotinus arises – as mentioned above – from a kind of overflowing from the fullness, and consequently we could almost say that it is literally "superfluous" – the whole inspiration of the path lies in leaving the world behind and returning to the One who is All. Plotinus is here in agreement with certain world-negative traditions of Hinduism, though not with Sri Aurobindo, who

---

[15] Purani, *Evening Talks with Sri Aurobindo* (1995), 120

sought to overcome them. For Sri Aurobindo it is in no way a contradiction or philosophical problem that a divine being which is already perfect and fulfilled, seeks to manifest itself in order to experience itself in Matter, which is at first darkened and later fully "enlightened". Here pertains the "logic of the infinite", as he once called it; "but if we insist on applying a finite logic to the Infinite, the omnipresent Reality will escape us."[16]

In concluding we may note that Sri Aurobindo had good reasons to doubt Krishnaprem's equating *Nous* with supermind, although there might be at least a spark of truth in it due to some remarkable affinity in a few aspects.

The *Nous* with Anaxagoras

Plotinus has written his texts in Greek, all of which have been preserved. The term *Nous* was already established in Presocratic times, it had some great importance especially in the thought of Anaxagoras (499-428 B.C.). The latter is well-known for having brought Greek philosophy from Asia Minor (where it had its origins) to Athens. He was in the tradition of the Ionic natural philosophers and tried to fathom the question of the primal ground of the world and of an ordering principle in the universe.

It was his conviction that "Something" can impossibly become out of Nothing or pass into Nothing. He rather believed that all Becoming and Vanishing are the mixing together or separating of some primal material in the form of an infinite number of small particles of various kinds, the homoeomeries, which are in themselves eternal and unchanging. The individual object originates from a specific mixture, and those elements that are predominantly represented, determine its character.

Sovereign above it as an ordering power is the *Nous* which gave the impulse for movement and separation in an originally immobile mass. In Fragment B 12 Anaxagoras describes the *Nous* as follows:

> ... Nous is infinite and self-ruled, and is mixed with nothing, but is

---

[16] *The Life Divine*, 337

alone, itself by itself... For it is the thinnest of all things and the purest, and it has all knowledge about everything and the greatest strength... And Nous had power over the whole revolution so that it began to revolve in the beginning... And Nous set in order all things that were to be, and all things that were and are not now and that are.[17]

In connection with the supermind Sri Aurobindo often speaks of Consciousness-Force. This term not only implies perfect knowledge, but also force of realization in the world of becoming. Therefore, Anaxagoras' statements are remarkable as a similar approach in this important aspect. In contrast to other natural philosophers such as Democritus, who reduces all occurence to a mere mechanism of atoms, Anaxagoras for the first time seeks to achieve a holistic vision, describing the universe from the viewpoint of a higher order. Johannes Hirschberger concludes that this specific vision could only be possible due to "a principle which is something logical as well as dynamical... Anaxagoras discovers this principle in Spirit [Nous], which is force of thinking as well as of will."[18]

Significant in this analysis is Hirschberger's describing the principle as "something dynamical", because Sri Aurobindo often uses the latter term in connection with his definition of supermind, as for instance in the following quotation: "There is an eternal dynamic Truth-consciousness beyond mind. This is what we call supermind or gnosis."[19] Furthermore, we read in *The Synthesis of Yoga*: "But the gnosis is not only light, it is force; it is creative knowledge, it is the self-effective truth of the divine Idea."[20]

The Gnosis

At this point we may note that Sri Aurobindo often uses the term Gnosis as a synonym for supermind, in the same way as Sanskrit Vijnana. Both words mean "deep knowledge" and are etymologically related via the Sanskrit root *jñā*, to know. As for Vijnana, he actually ascribes

---

[17] Trl. J. Burnet.
[18] *Geschichte der Philosophie*, vol. I, 49
[19] *Essays Divine and Human*, 363
[20] *The Synthesis of Yoga*, 484

a "supramental" meaning to this term in the Upanishads, but it appears uncertain whether he assumed in the same way that the Greek term carried this meaning in some sources. In the course of centuries it was used with manifold meanings.

There seems to be no text in which Sri Aurobindo directly addresses this topic, but there is at least an indirect hint suggesting the reasons for the use of Gnosis as a synonym for supermind. It is found in the second quotation at the beginning of this chapter, where Sri Aurobindo declares thoughts of the Upanishads to be "the profoundest part" of Gnosticism. Possibly he assumes that there was an intercultural exchange in whose course some Indian knowledge was being transferred to the West. We had already presented a statement in the preceding chapter in which he declared, "something of the philosophy of India got through by means of Pythagoras and others."[21]

Another reading might be that from Sri Aurobindo's viewpoint the early European mystics were living in an experience similar to that of the Indian Rishis of ancient times, having access to a comparable inspiration, which would also explain the high status of the term Gnosis in his writings.

Finally, a few words on the gnostic movement as such: characteristic of its philosophy in the post-Christian era was a turning towards mysticism, the use of Platonic, Stoic and Pythagorean elements of teaching, a fathoming of ultimate questions such as life after death and the pursuit of salvation not through faith, but through knowledge of God or knowledge of the world of the suprasensuous – the Gnosis.

---

[21] *Letters on Poetry and Art*, 520

F.W. Schelling

5

Schelling and his Natural Philosophy

History as a whole is a progressive, gradually self-disclosing revelation of the Absolute.[1]

F.W.J. Schelling

Therefore for Schelling every natural being – a tree, an animal, even a piece of mineral – is not only an observable object of the external world, but at the same time an expression of the divine life present in it. Nature is "the secret God".[2]

Wilhelm Weischedel

If it be true that Spirit is involved in Matter and apparent Nature is secret God, then the manifestation of the divine in himself and the realisation of God within and without are the highest and most legitimate aim possible to man upon earth.[3]

Sri Aurobindo

Fichte, Schelling[4] and Hegel are the three great names of German idealism, with Schelling occupying a position closest to Sri Aurobindo. However, the latter does not mention him anywhere in his works, letters or talks, whereas Hegel is referred to several times. Fichte is briefly mentioned in a single passage as an important philosopher, along with Kant, Hegel and Nietzsche.[5]

As a rule, in the Indian secondary literature on Sri Aurobindo Hegel alone is considered, but a few Western authors are also aware of

---

[1] *System des transzendenten Idealismus*, Leipzig 1979, p. 251
[2] *Die philosophische Hintertreppe*, München 2004, p. 205.
[3] *The Life Divine*, 6
[4] To be pronounced as *shelling*.
[5] *The Human Cycle*, 41

Schelling's relevance. Thus, Ken Wilber notes in a Preface that, apart from Sri Aurobindo, a few other thinkers such as Schelling and Hegel had realized "that evolution is basically Spirit-in-action... But nobody combined both philosophical brilliance and a profoundly enlightened consciousness the way Aurobindo did. His enlightenment informed his philosophy; his philosophy gave substance to his enlightenment; and that combination has been rarely equalled, in this or any time."[6]

Klaus J. Bracker too refers to Schelling in his comparative study on Sri Aurobindo and Rudolf Steiner. In a chapter on Evolution and Egoity he works out some significant points and shows especially that Schelling "in his natural philosophy overcame all static concepts in favour of his so-called 'dynamic evolution', allowing new developments."[7]

Furthermore, in an article on evolutionary spirituality Tom Huston has paid tribute to Schelling, among others, stating that he initiated a remarkable reunification of science and spirituality with his romantic, but thorough rational mind. Houston elaborates:

> Schelling proposed an alternative to the encroaching materialism so dreaded by his Romantic friends: an *evolutionary idealism*. As the opposite of materialism, the philosophy of idealism held that consciousness, not matter, was the ultimate basis of reality. And once combined with a scientific understanding of evolution, Schelling realized, idealism would represent a force with which all serious thinkers of the Enlightenment would have to contend.[8]

Actually, we may argue that never before nor thereafter, German philosophy came so close to Sri Aurobindo's thought as in Schelling's idealism. We found commentaries in the Net whose authors assume with certainty that Sri Aurobindo must have studied intensively Schelling's writings, as the convergences are so obvious. However, as mentioned above, there is no evidence for it. But this does not exclude the possibility that he had chanced upon one or the other thought in the

---

[6] A.S. Dalal, *A Greater Psychology. An Introduction to the Psychological Thought of Sri Aurobindo.* New York 2001, Foreword Ken Wilber, p. vii
[7] *Veda und lebendiger Logos*, Frankfurt 2014, 113-14
[8] *tomhuston.com / a brief history of evolutionary spirituality*. Retrieved on 25-5-2015

few titles of secondary literature which he may have read on the subject of philosophy; in one of his letters he mentions a little book on Hegel.[9] But basically convergences might be explained by the fact that Vedantic influences in Sri Aurobindo's writings meet with Neo-Platonic influences in Schelling's writings, resulting in kindred statements. Sri Aurobindo himself had pointed out that the philosophy of the Upanishads is closely related to Neo-Platonism.[10]

Schelling's life and work

Friedrich Wilhelm Joseph Ritter von Schelling (1775-1854) was born in the family of a Protestant pastor in South West Germany. His father was a renowned orientalist, furthering at an early stage the manifold interests of his precocious son. The latter studied Christian theology in Tübingen jointly with F. Hölderlin and G.W.F. Hegel, establishing a fruitful friendship with them. He read intensively the writings of Spinoza and Kant and wrote his M.A. thesis in 1792 on the origin of evil. Spinoza was later to become an important influence in his philosophy, in the same way as Giordano Bruno.

However, at first it was Fichte's philosophy which had priority for him. Fichte was teaching at Jena at that time, advocating his subjective idealism. Schelling felt attracted to this doctrine, but as his own development progressed, he could no more identify with it and broke with Fichte after the turn of the century. Having a tremendous aspiration for learning, he took up studies of mathematics, sciences and medicine after completing his theological course. He made the acquaintance of Goethe and Schiller and published a first natural philosophical writing in 1797. At the end of the same year he met the poet Novalis, who – as Schelling's biographer Jochen Kirchhoff has pointed out – "was deeply inspired (like Hölderlin and Hegel) by the idea of being on the threshold of a new era which would bring a new philosophy, even a new religion."[11]

A year later he went to Dresden where he got access to the circle of early Romantics around the Schlegel brothers. They too had a kind of

---
[9] See next chapter, with further remarks on this subject.
[10] See his quotation at the beginning of the chapter "Plotinus".
[11] *Schelling*, Reinbek 2000, p. 28

New Age awareness, the feeling that a new epoch would usher in a living synthesis of all creative endeavours. The term "synthesis" is quite significant here, because it also plays a major role in Sri Aurobindo's integral thought. When he started the journal *Arya* with Mirra Alfassa in 1914, the aim was described as "the formation of a vast synthesis of knowledge, harmonising the diverse religious traditions of humanity, occidental as well as oriental."[12]

Novalis, L. Tieck and F.D.E. Schleiermacher belonged to this circle of very open-minded literary figures, offering Schelling a highly conducive setting for his own development. New research became possible now, as the Schlegel brothers were pioneers of Sanskrit studies in Germany, preparing among others the first translation of the Bhagavadgita in Latin and German. Thus, Schelling had early access to hitherto little-known texts, which he explored indefatigably with his receptive mind. Later on, in some lectures, he was to focus extensively on Indian subjects and especially the Bhagavadgita. In 1798 he became professor in Jena with the support of Goethe, who held him in great esteem, and published some more writings on natural philosophy and idealism, as well as a Socratic dialogue titled *Bruno or on the Natural and Divine Principle of Things*.

There followed stays in Würzburg and Munich where he studied particularly the Theosophical philosophy of Jacob Böhme and worked several years on his important treatise *Philosophy of the Ages*, which however was never completed. In his writing *Philosophy and Religion* he deals with subjects such as reincarnation and at this stage becomes "the spokesman of a Romantic era which aims at religious revival, an inclusion of the spiritual in philosophy."[13]

After some more changes of locality Schelling finally arrives in Berlin in 1841, where he is invited to take over the vacant chair of Hegel, who had died in 1831. Over time, the latter had taken up some philosophical positions different from those of Schelling and attained great academic fame. Schelling's succession created some interest at the beginning, but he could not fulfil the high expectations, which is why students and other listeners stayed away more and more. As a

---

[12] Quoted in: W. Huchzermeyer, Sri Aurobindo, Delhi 2013, p. 151
[13] J. Kirchhoff, *Schelling*, 41

consequence, after a while he stopped his lectures, but continued living and working in Berlin. In 1854 he died while taking a cure in Switzerland.

Schelling's Indian studies

Before discussing Schelling's natural philosophy, which is particularly relevant for a comparison with Sri Aurobindo's thought, we will have a look at his Indian studies. They reveal his wide mind, his ability to take up and assimilate easily thoughts of a foreign culture – a challenge which many other great minds failed to meet adequately. In his title *The Conspiracy of Life – Meditations on Schelling and His Time*[14] Jason M. Wirth mentions Schelling's writing *Philosophy of Mythology* (1842), containing brilliant analyses of different oriental traditions (including the Indian), and notes:

> What is immediately striking about Schelling's analysis of India is its utter lack of the condescension that typified the nineteenth-century reception of India, from English colonial interests to Christian proselytizing interests to Max Müller's refusal to visit India. Between the Scylla and Charybdis of exoticism and Orientalism, Schelling found in India one of the world's great philosophical traditions.[15]

Hegel was one of those who looked down on India, considering it a relict left behind by the world-spirit in its journey to self-revelation. He believed that the Indians, having an inclination to focus on an abstract Infinite, were unable to think historically and therefore also lacked the capacity for a political and philosophical renewal. But he also thought that they had an inclination to deify everything, "their imagination makes everything into a god."[16] Wirth aptly comments on Hegel's convictions: "Nowhere does one find the stinginess of Hegel... more apparent than in his repudiation of India, and, by way of the starkest of contrasts, the deification not of all things, but of the

---

[14] New York, 2003
[15] *The Conspiracy of Life*. Meditations on Schelling and His Time. New York 2003, p. 222
[16] Quoted in ibid., 223

Prussian state."[17]

In the 22nd lecture of the series *Philosophy of Mythology* Schelling also reflects on the term yoga. It is an interesting moment in time, when the cultural avant-garde of Western Europe becomes for the first time aware of the importance of this Sanskrit word and tries to explore its meaning. Schelling mentions the attempts of Schlegel and others to find an appropriate German translation such as *Einheit* or *Andacht*,[18] but rejects them as inadequate.

> I wonder why nobody thought of *Innigkeit*, which implies the state of innerness, of being in oneself, in one's depth... and at the same time the idea of oneness and unity.[19]

Schelling's proposal is quite brilliant, but his treatise on the Bhagavadgita as a whole is in many respects only of historical interest today, although it addresses some deep philosophical issues. Wirth has commented on the lectures in his above-mentioned title and also adduces some quotations from Sri Aurobindo's *Essays on the Gita* for throwing more light on the subject. His résumé on Schelling's Indian studies is that they are certainly not without errors and that we cannot go along with all of his interpretations; but Wirth believes it is worth nonetheless "to indicate the richness of Schelling's opening into these [Indian] traditions."[20]

We may assume that Schelling had early access to the English Bhagavadgita translation of Charles Wilkens which came to Europe in 1785, because already in 1795 we come across, in his writing *Of the I as the Principle of Philosophy*,[21] the idea of a melting of the individual I with the Absolute through an overcoming of *maya*, illusion, which gives us the suggestion of multiplicity. These are ideas which remind us rather of Shankara and his Advaita Vedanta, but the latter sources were not yet accessible at that time. The Latin Gita translation of Au-

---

[17] Ibid., 223
[18] Union, devotion, meditation.
[19] *Schellings sämtliche Werke,* Stuttgart-Augsburg 1856-61, XII, 488. It is interesting to note that in modern German *Innigkeit* means intimacy or ardency and the notion of oneness, today *Einigkeit*, is not suggested any more.
[20] *The Conspiracy of Life,* 220
[21] *Vom Ich als Prinzip der Philosophie*, also translated as "Of the Ego..." or „Of the Self...".

gust Wilhelm von Schlegel was published only in 1823, but Schelling knew some other old Indian texts as early as 1802.

The evolutionary philosophy of Sri Aurobindo

> The Spirit shall look out through Matter's gaze
> And Matter shall reveal the Spirit's face.[22]

Sri Aurobindo had a spiritual collaborator, Mirra Alfassa (1878-1973), who met him first in Pondicherry in 1914 and shared his path of integral yoga permanently from 1920 onwards. She was French with Turkish-Egyptian roots and had a deep knowledge of the esoteric, spiritual and wisdom traditions of the world. In the Sri Aurobindo Ashram she was called "the Mother", and it was her part to guide the inmates in their daily life, trying to realize the yoga developed by Sri Aurobindo, on a practical plane.

During the 1950ies she regularly addressed the students of the Ashram's International Centre of Education, answering their manifold questions. In one of these *Entretiens* she presented with great clarity and in simple language the natural philosophy of Sri Aurobindo, which was also her own. In the following pages we will look at some extracts of this text, with headings added to the individual passages to bring out their specific content.

Return to the divine origin – the intention of Nature
Hidden in the depths, at the core of matter, there is the Divine Presence and... the whole terrestrial evolution is made to prepare the return of the creation to its origin, to this Divine Presence which is at the centre of everything – that is the intention of Nature.

The universe as an objectivisation of the Supreme
The universe is an objectivisation of the Supreme, as if He had objectivised himself outside of himself in order to see himself, to live himself, to know himself, and so that there might be an existence and a consciousness capable of recognising him as their origin and uniting

---

[22] *Savitri*, 709

consciously with him to manifest him in the becoming.

The special position of the earth
The earth is a kind of symbolic crystallisation of universal life, a reduction, a concentration, so that the work of evolution may be easier to do and follow. And if we see the history of the earth, we can understand why the universe has been created. It is the Supreme growing aware of himself in an eternal Becoming; and the goal is the union of the created with the Creator, a union that is conscious, willing and free, in the Manifestation.

The secret of Nature
That is the secret of Nature. Nature is the executive Force, it is she who does the work. And she takes up this creation, which appears to be totally inconscient but which contains the Supreme Consciousness and sole Reality and she works so that all this can develop, become self-aware and realise itself fully. But she does not show it from the very beginning. It develops gradually, and that is why at the start it is a secret which will be unveiled as it nears the end. And man has reached a point in the evolution high enough for this secret to be unveiled and for what was done in an apparent inconscience to be done consciously, willingly, and therefore much more rapidly and in the joy of realisation.

The conscious evolutionary collaboration of humans
In man one can already see that the spiritual reality is being developed and that it is going to express itself totally and freely. Formerly, in the animal and the plant, it was... necessary to be very clear-sighted to see it, but man is himself conscious of the spiritual reality, at least in the higher part of his human existence. Man is beginning to know what the Supreme Origin wants of him and is collaborating in carrying it out. Nature wants the creation to become conscious of being the Creator himself in an objectivisation, that is to say, there is no difference between the Creator and the Creation, and the goal is a conscious and realised union. That is the secret of Nature.[23]

---

[23] *Collected Works of the Mother*, 9, 321-22

Here ends the Mother's text from her *Talks* with the students; it will be supplemented in what follows by some passages from Sri Aurobindo's *The Life Divine*. As a source for our exposition, we choose chapter 24, Book 2, The Evolution of the Spiritual Man. In this chapter Sri Aurobindo uses a special stylistic device for his "narrative": he creates an imaginary eye witness who follows the becoming of creation from the first beginning, and describes how this witness experiences the different stages. Thus we get something like a living report of creation, which in the following will be briefly summarized.

In the initial stage the witness would have seen an energy appearing out of a vast abyss of an apparent non-existence, creating Matter and the material world, bringing forth out of the infinity of the inconscient an infinite universe or even a system of numberless universes. But it would have appeared to him like a giant spectacle without any obvious meaning or purpose. At this stage it would have seemed impossible for him to imagine that in this infinite desert there would eventually originate life and mind or an awakening soul.

If the same witness would have looked again at this scene after many ages, he would have registered at least in a small corner of the universe, the earth, the phenomenon of life in matter, without however understanding anything, because evolutionary nature still kept her secret hidden. He would have perceived a colourful dab in the desert, where creation enjoys the act of endless creating. He would have glimpsed the first beginnings of a mind, but the latter only in the service of the vital energy in order to organise its impulses more efficiently for attack, defence and self-fulfilment.

At this point he could not have guessed what would happen in the next stage: the genesis of thinking humans, developing a conscious intelligence and constructing tools with its support, building houses and cities with giant structures, becoming active in sciences, humanities and arts. The principle of Mind is now firmly established as an evolutionary stage and takes over the lead of life.

But even at this stage the witness would not have recognized the hidden action of the Spirit or even admitted it as a possibility, but would have interpreted the conscious activity of the brain cells as an exceptional phenomenon on earth which was nothing but a tiny point in the infinity of an inanimate universe. Only the witness who casts a look at the scene "at the end of the story" would comprehend the whole miracle, recognizing the emergence of the Spirit involved in the inconscience, which has created all manifestation for its own habitation.

But then Sri Aurobindo adds that a more conscious witness might have discovered already at an early stage the clue for understanding the process of evolution. For step by step the veil of the secret is lifted, and there are hints indicating the presence of an underlying spiritual consciousness trying to emerge. This is the process:

> As plant life contains in itself the obscure possibility of the conscious animal, as the animal-mind is astir with the movements of feeling and perception and the rudiments of conception that are the first ground for man the thinker, so man the mental being is sublimated by the endeavour of the evolutionary Energy to develop out of him the spiritual man, the fully conscious being, man exceeding his first material self and discoverer of his true self and highest nature.[24]

The evolution of spiritual man, Sri Aurobindo continues, can only be possible if we assume the existence of a Spirit as something basically different from Mind and beyond it:

> Spirit is a final evolutionary emergence because it is the original involutionary element and factor. Evolution is an inverse action of the involution: what is an ultimate and last derivation in the involution [Matter] is the first to appear in the evolution; what was original and primal in the involution [Spirit] is in the evolution the last and supreme emergence.[25]

To experience the Spirit or Soul in their true form is difficult in the early stages of awakening. Only "when there is a complete silence in the being…, then we can become aware of a Self, a spiritual substance of our being, an existence exceeding even the soul-individuality." It is an existence with a cosmic wideness and transcendent height, going beyond all

---

[24] *The Life Divine*, 883-84
[25] Ibid., 885-86

limits. "It is these liberations of the spiritual part in us which are the decisive step of the spiritual evolution in Nature."[26]

So we may resume: for Sri Aurobindo evolution is marked by the gradual emergence of the principles of Matter, Life, Mind, Spirit. However, the individual rungs on the ladder are not left behind, but further developed in the framework of the next higher step and finally fulfilled by the Spirit; in this sense it is an integral vision.

But once the stage of the *spiritual* evolution has been reached, it can proceed in different directions. Thus, an individual may turn his back on the universe and manifestation after a full realization of the supreme Self by entering into the self-dissolution of Nirvana. Sri Aurobindo has confirmed this as an option in his writings, but he refused to accept it for himself and his path. He was advocating a fulfilled divine life on earth, made possible through supermind as an intermediary power between the two spheres of the infinite spirit and the finite manifestation.

Schelling's natural philosophy

> Nature shall be the visible spirit, the spirit shall be the invisible Nature.[27]
> History is an epic composed in the mind of God.[28]

Schelling's natural philosophy was formulated particularly in a series of writings between 1797 and 1806, not in the form of a closed system, but in the shape of ever new drafts and concepts. Following Fichte, whom he at first admired, he considers the human "I" as the truly real, as highest principle, the "absolute I" in which all other reality exists only as an imagination.

But after some time he leaves behind this approach, by discovering a deeper dimension of the human "I" and calling it "the Eternal within us". This dimension becomes accessible to him through "intellectual

---

[26] Ibid., 887
[27] *Schellings Sämtliche Werke*, II, 56
[28] Ibid., VI, 57

vision",[29] through introspection:

> We all have a secret, wonderful capacity inside us to withdraw from the flux of time into our inmost Self that is unrobed of everything coming to us from outside, and there to contemplate the eternal in us in the form of immutability. This vision is the innermost and most personal experience upon which everything we know and believe of the extrasensory world alone depends... This intellectual vision comes to pass where we cease to be an object for ourselves, where, withdrawn within itself, the observing Self is identical with the observed. In this moment of vision time and duration vanish for us; it is not we who are in time, but time is in us – or rather not time, but pure absolute identity in us.[30]

It is a powerful spiritual vision unfolding here, reminding us of the experience of the Atman described in the Upanishads, that is to say the immortal Self, one with the Brahman, the Absolute. This is in line with Schelling's objective to comprehend the reality as an organic whole, which can only be possible from the perspective of the Absolute. The latter is the supreme Divine, pervading all existence as infinite life – it is not, however, the Christian Creator-God, facing his own creation like an external object.

Schelling disassociates himself from the growing materialistic approach that considers nature as an object for the use of humans and has importance only insofar as it has value for them. In contrast, Herder and Goethe had inspired a new feeling for nature recognising its vitality and the creative forces in it. The philosopher and biographer Jochen Kirchhoff sums up Schelling's position as follows: "His protest is directed against the abstraction of mathematical science, divesting nature of its life, and against a philosophy aiming at a splitting of spirit and nature. From his viewpoint, both [approaches] are similar in character, having the same effects. Both deny the living existence of the divine and spirit-informed nature, and they are there-

---

[29] Intellektuelle Anschauung, The German word, derived from *anschauen*, to view, may also be translated as intuition or perception.
[30] *Schellings sämtliche Werke*, I, 318-19

fore for Schelling symptoms of a refusal to take the reality as it is."[31] However, Schelling himself is reproached by some critics as being a romantic dreamer, which he rejects by pointing out that this accusation is common in the cultural history vis-à-vis those thinkers whose thought is not understood by other scholars.

What really connects Schelling with Sri Aurobindo, is the basic openness to the sciences and their knowledge, but combined with a refusal to be overwhelmed by them and to make them the centre of our world-view. For both thinkers the objective is to put the findings in their proper place, giving them their right position in the total structure. With great foresight Schelling realized the dangers of a too one-sided focussing on abstract analytical thought and technical progress at the cost of nature:

> No human being has so far been able to bridle nature, and if Fichte says that nature is to be livened up in its own development through reasonable life, we may retort that precisely the contrary is the case, for whenever nature serves human purposes, it is being killed.[32]

Now we may enquire what is Schelling's view of nature and its becoming. We had given above a quotation from the Mother's works in which she speaks of a secret of nature that is to be unveiled. Similarly, Schelling says:

> What we call nature is a poem hidden in a secret wonderful script. But the riddle could be disclosed, if we could recognize in it the odyssey of the spirit which, wonderfully deluded, itself seeking itself, flees from itself; for through the world of senses glimpses only the meaning as through words as it were, glimpses only, through a half-translucent fog, the land of fantasia for which we aspire.

What Schelling has in mind and tries to work out in ever new approaches, is a powerful concept: "We are in a position now... to state that actually the whole process of world creation... is nothing else

---

[31] J. Kirchhoff, *Schelling*, 60
[32] *Schellings sämtliche Werke*, VII, 17

than the process of the perfect becoming conscious, the perfect personalization of God."[33] So we find that for him creation is an unfolding of the Absolute in Time, at the end of which there is – as Kirchhoff resumes – "the resolution of the unconscious (in the Divine and in Nature) or its relocation into unity, respectively."[34]

In his writing *The Ages of the World* Schelling tried from 1810 to explore the different stages of the self-revelation of the Divine and to interpret its workings in the world, especially in the form of historical processes. It is significant that he considers the earth "as a scene of the God-made occurrence", as Kirchhoff formulates it, and that the cosmos as a whole is put in the rear. It is exactly in the restriction to finiteness "that Schelling has seen the reality of divine action since *The Ages of the World*."[35] We may compare this with a statement of the Mother quoted above: "The earth is a kind of symbolic crystallisation of universal life, a reduction, a concentration, so that the work of evolution may be easier to do and follow."

In Schelling's vision nature is like a ladder progressively developing towards ever higher creations. What Sri Aurobindo terms Matter, Life, Mind, is similarly seen by Schelling, although described with a partially different terminology. He believes that every natural product comes into being through the interplay of polarities, as for instance in the inorganic field of magnetism and electricity or in the organic field of the male and female. As soon as the spirit awakens in humans and starts reflecting, a new stage in world history and God-genesis begins, at the end of which "God shall be", as Schelling said. He believes that reason (*Vernunft*) will play a special role in this second phase of evolution:

> Therefore, the so-called dead nature is nothing else than immature intelligence so that the intelligent character always shines through, still unconsciously, in its phenomena. The highest goal of nature – to become completely objective to itself – is reached by it only through its highest and ultimate reflection, which is none other than man or, more generally, it is that which we call reason; for through it nature com-

---

[33] Ibid., VII, 433
[34] J. Kirchhoff, *Schelling*, 46
[35] Ibid., 47

pletely returns within itself; and it becomes evident that nature originally is identical with what is known in us as intelligence and the conscious.[36]

As Sri Aurobindo once remarked with reference to Plotinus, other philosophers did not develop the same kind of differentiations as he did, such as mind, overmind, supermind etc. But we may assume that "intelligence" and "the conscious" do refer to a higher plane than pure mind; what is meant is *Geist* in its widest sense. Consequently, Kirchhoff comments: "According to Schelling, in the knowing of reason the Divine is always present. The universe is the self-revelation of God, the self-viewing of the Absolute in which reason has a living participation."

For Sri Aurobindo, the mental plane is a problematic intermediary stage, as the original harmony of nature gets lost here without being replaced by a higher one. It is only on the planes beyond mind that the harmony is re-established in a higher form through an enlightened, integral consciousness. Similarly, Schelling too comprehends natural philosophy as "recovery of the former union of humans with nature on a higher plane..., as the retrieval of harmony of humans and cosmos after a long phase of alienation and separation", as Kirchhoff points out.[37]

Real-Idealism

Schelling has coined the term *Real-Idealismus*, which is of special interest in the context of comparative studies with Sri Aurobindo, because it calls up the association with the latter's Real Idea – a term he has used in *The Life Divine*. In the following we repeat a text already given in chapter 3:

> The view I am presenting goes farther in idealism; it sees the creative Idea as Real-Idea, that is to say, a power of Conscious-Force expressive of real being, born out of real being and partaking of its nature

---

[36] Schelling, quoted in: J. Hirschberger, *Geschichte der Philosophie*, II, 380
[37] J. Kirchhoff, *Schelling*, 76

and neither a child of the Void nor a weaver of fictions. It is conscious Reality throwing itself into mutable forms of its own imperishable and immutable substance. The world is therefore not a figment of conception in the universal Mind, but a conscious birth of that which is beyond Mind into forms of itself.[38]

For Schelling, the outer world "lies open before us to rediscover in it the history of our spirit." "Nature shall be the visible spirit, spirit shall be the invisible nature. So it is here, in the absolute identity of the spirit in us and nature outside us, that the problem of the possibility of a nature external to us has to be resolved."[39]

As for Sri Aurobindo, so for Schelling too the term "unity", *Einheit*, is of central importance: unity of nature and spirit, being and consciousness for which he coined the term Real-Idealism or Identity Philosophy, "and he combined with it the substantial self-assurance of having achieved that great intellectual synthesis which would be henceforth the measure of all philosophy. It was the effort of preserving the idealistic primate of the spirit, of freedom and will without losing the living fullness of objective existence."[40] Schelling himself once remarked on this synthesis: "Idealism is the soul of philosophy; realism its body; only both of them together make a living whole. Never can the latter provide the principle, but it must be the ground and the means in which the first realises itself."[41]

Schelling also seems to come very close to Sri Aurobindo's concept of a dynamic, world-active truth-consciousness, when he writes:

The Godlike universe is not only the spoken word of God, *but itself that which speaks,* not that which is created, but that which itself creates and reveals itself in an infinite way.[42]

We may compare this statement with the following of the American scholar Steve Odin in an article on Sri Aurobindo and Hegel. The

---

[38] *The Life Divine*, 125
[39] *Schellings sämtliche Werke*, I, 383; II, 56
[40] J. Kirchhoff, *Schelling*, 76
[41] *Schellings sämtliche Werke,*, 330
[42] Ibid., VII, 162

passage is treating Sri Aurobindo's concept of the Absolute as living Spirit. Odin addresses an important subject here which will be further discussed in the next chapter:

> The historical self-unfolding of Spirit at the cosmic level is not predetermined, mechanistic or purely continuous, but is an emergent process which is being perpetually animated and restructured by new evolutionary principles descending from the supramental planes.[43]

Brilliantly inspired also appears to be Schelling's following passage on the interrelation between micro- and macrocosm and infinity:

> In every organic being, even in the smallest portion of it, you recognize the actual infinity and the oneness each for themselves and nevertheless as one. But every atom of matter is an equally infinite world as the whole universe; in the smallest portion resounds the eternal word of the divine relationship.[44]

We complete this section on Real-Idealism and Real-Idea with a lengthy quotation of Schelling, taken from his writing titled *General Overview of the Latest Philosophical Literature* (1797). It summarizes in a lucid manner the key ideas of his natural and developmental philosophy:

> In purposiveness, form and matter, concept and intuition interpenetrate. This is precisely the character of the spirit in which the Ideal and the Real are absolutely united. Therefore, there is something symbolic in every organization, and every plant is so to speak the intertwined delineation[45] of the soul.[46] As there is in our spirit an infinite striving to

---

[43] *Sri Aurobindo and Hegel on the Involution-Evolution of Absolute Spirit*. Philosophy East and West, Vol. 31, No. 2, pp. 179-191. University of Hawai, 1981
[44] *Schellings sämtliche Werke*, VII, 180
[45] Der verschlungene Zug der Seele. "Zug" can also mean trait.
[46] In this context we feel reminded of the Mother's interpretations of flowers. She said that "flowers speak to us when we know how to listen to them. It is a subtle and fragrant language." Thus she gave specific meanings to more than 900 flowers, such as aspiration, hope, sincerity, love, joy, adoration etc., by trying to feel their respective vibrations. The various meanings have been published in the title *The Spiritual Significance of Flowers* (Pondicherry, Sri Aurobindo Ashram).

organize itself, so also in the external world there must reveal itself a general tendency towards organization. Such indeed is the case. The system of the world is a kind of organization which has developed from a common centre...

From bits of moss in which hardly any visible trace of organization is left, to the noblest form, which seems to have cast off the chains of matter, it is one and the same drive that governs. It seems to operate according to one and the same ideal of purposiveness and presses forward into infinity, trying to express one and the same archetype, the pure form of our mind. No organization would be conceivable without productive force. I would like to know how such a force would enter matter, if we regard the latter as a thing in itself. We need no longer be hesitant in our claims, there cannot be any doubt about what happens daily before our eyes. There is a productive force in things external to us. But this kind of force is only the force of a spirit... The gradated chain of organizations and the transition from the inanimate to animate nature clearly indicates a productive force which only gradually develops towards full freedom.[47]

Therefore, life necessarily exists in nature. Just as there is a gradated chain of organizations, there will also be a gradated chain of life. Only gradually the spirit approximates its own nature. It is necessary that it appears for itself as an external form, namely as organized, animated matter. For only life is the visible analogue of the spirit.[48]

Thus, for Schelling the universe is a living organism, a living work of art.[49] It is the self-revelation of God, at the same time also his self-viewing and self-realization. Schelling perceives a unity of existence and consciousness and a development in the form of a dynamic sequence of stages. Ultimately, everything originates from an *Urbild*, archetype, the highest form of consciousness, *the* Real-Idea as it were. However, there is one question that still remains to be answered: What is the deeper intention behind the self-revelation of the Absolute in the

---

[47] *Schellings sämtliche Werke*, I, 386-87
[48] Ibid., I, 388
[49] Art as such has a great importance in Schelling's philosophy, he considers it as the highest in the field of the spirit: "Art is paramount to the philosopher... it is art alone which can succeed in objectifying with universality what the philosopher is able to present in a merely subjective fashion." (*Schellings sämtliche Werke*, III, 628)

finite world? In the following passage of his writing *Philosophy and Religion* (1804) Schelling refers to this question in a way reminiscent of Neo-Platonic thought:

> The great intention of the universe and its history is no other than the perfected reconciliation and redissolution into Absoluteness.
> The great intention of the whole world manifestation thus expresses itself in history. The ideas, the spirits had to fall from their inner centre, introduce themselves into particularity, in the nature of the general sphere of the fall, so that afterwards, as particular beings, they could return into the indifference[50] and, reconciled to it, be in it without disturbing it.[51]

Evil and the anti-divine

This takes us to the subject of the "fall" into finiteness and the anti-divine forces experienced there, causing pain and suffering. Schelling had initially excluded this subject in his early writings on natural philosophy, for evil and the anti-divine are phenomena which – at least at first sight – appear to be incompatible with the vision of the world as a perfect divine work of art. But he was too deep and passionate a thinker to bypass this problem. Since 1808 he began once more to study intensively Jakob Böhme (1575-1624) and got inspiration for his readings from mystic circles around F.C. Oetinger. Böhme had conceived an *Ungrund*, unground, which is a new word creation also in German, analogous to *Urgrund* or primal ground. The unground has a pressing blind will, but is initially self-reposed as silence, bliss and freedom. It is only with the movement from Nothing to Something, connected with the individualisation, that the darkening and the conflict of opposites comes about.

Schelling conceives a rupture in the One Absolute, perceives a Fall in the unground and a primal evil. In the latter originates all that is evil and imperfect in the world, whereas the beautiful and the good is based on the luminous will in God, the Logos. The Absolute is now at

---

[50] Schelling uses the term *Indifferenz* in the sense of the coinciding of nature and spirit in the Absolute.
[51] *Schellings sämtliche Werke*, VI, 43; 57

the same time luminous primal ground and darkened unground, with humans having the freedom of making their choice. From this arises the possibility of guilt and the reality of life with the battle between good and evil. But in the awakened humans there is an aspiration for the light and therefore they become aware when they go astray, making a decision for the evil, and ultimately they strive for the Truth and a return to God. Johannes Hirschberger summarizes this philosophical approach as follows:

> The absolute Self enters a process of becoming: at first the blind will is still slumbering, God has not yet unfolded and still encloses his potentialities (*deus implicitus*); but then the blind will awakens and the primal Fall in God occurs; as a consequence there is the inclusion of evil in the world and in humans; they are not any more entirely thoughts of God; there arises the battle between light and darkness; it ends with the victory of the light, after the evil too has been pervaded by the divine Spirit and thus released. It is only now that God has completely revealed himself, he is – as Oetinger and similarly Cusanus said – a *deus explicitus* and has thereby also attained his self-perfection.[52]

Thus Schelling arrives, in spite of a full inclusion of the "shadow" and in spite of many bitter moments of despairing of the world and its tragic events, at a kind of evolutionary confidence, which he has in common with Sri Aurobindo whose philosophical treatment of the anti-divine we present next.

Sri Aurobindo on the anti-divine

Sri Aurobindo has dealt with the darker side of existence at every stage of his inner and outer path. He treats this subject in many of his texts, in his spiritual epic *Savitri* and in his philosophical main work *The Life Divine* and other essays. One of the chapters in the latter work is titled *The Origin and Remedy of Falsehood, Error, Wrong*

---

[52] *Geschichte der Philosophie*, II, 390

and Evil.[53]

If we analyse his approach, we realize that it is similar to that of J. Hirschberger described above, using the terms *deus implicitus* and *deus explicitus*, that is to say the Divine still deeply involved, slumbering, and the Divine emerged, awakened. Where Böhme and Schelling posit an unground, locating in it the origin of the anti-divine, Sri Aurobindo conceives an Inconscience as source of the anti-divine. However, he emphasizes that it is not established as self-existent element in the supreme Absolute:

> Falsehood and Evil are, unlike Truth and Good, very clearly results of the Ignorance and cannot exist where there is no Ignorance: they can have no self-existence in the Divine being... there can therefore be no absolute of falsehood, no absolute of evil; these things are a by-product of the world-movement: the sombre flowers of falsehood and suffering and evil have their root in the black soil of the Inconscient.

And Sri Aurobindo continues, by opening a perspective for the evolutionary future:

> On the other hand, there is no such intrinsic obstacle to the absoluteness of Truth and Good: the relativity of truth and error, good and evil is a fact of our experience, but it is similarly a by-product, it is not a permanent factor native to existence; for it is true only of the valuations made by the human consciousness, true only of our partial knowledge and partial ignorance.[54]

Through the manifestation the Divine has thrown a veil on itself as it were, limiting its infinity and thereby creating a *temporary* sphere of suffering and evil. For in the early stages of evolution progress comes about through the opposition of forces, and in its wake struggle, conflict and war. When the human consciousness awakens and when first rays of the light of the truth reach it, the perception of evil is born, and the perception of the anti-divine that resists any progress towards the

---

[53] Book 2, Part 1, chapter 14
[54] *The Life Divine*, 620

Supreme. In mythology the counterforces are depicted as demons, called Asuras in the ancient Sanskrit texts. The epic Mahabharata calls them "the elder brothers of the Gods",[55] because at a primal stage of creation they have turned away in revolt from the Supreme One in order to follow their own will. In some circumstances they are able to develop tremendous power which however remains limited nonetheless and cannot touch the infinity of the Absolute.

Now, as long as the evolution proceeds in Ignorance and in the narrow ego-consciousness, all development is accompanied by the experience of suffering and evil:

> A limited consciousness growing out of nescience is the source of error, a personal attachment to the limitation and the error born of it the source of falsity, a wrong consciousness governed by the life-ego the source of evil. But it is evident that their relative existence is only a phenomenon thrown up by the cosmic Force in its drive towards evolutionary self-expression, and it is there that we have to look for the significance of the phenomenon.[56]

The individual ego seeks self-fulfilment and self-aggrandisement, but on a deeper level it has behind itself the true spiritual Self. The latter at first leaves the egos their free scope and works out secretly and in the long run some progress out of the often painful opposition of forces. But as a growing number of humans feel this kind of evolution to be dissatisfying or even unbearable, a new step with new laws is being prepared:

> The true solution can intervene only when by our spiritual growth we can become one self with all beings, know them as part of our self, deal with them as if they were our other selves; for then the division is healed...[57]

It is only when humans attain a highest truth-consciousness of unity in which all things spontaneously find their right place, that an evolution

---

[55] Mbhr. 3.92.6, Pune Critical Edition.
[56] *The Life Divine*, 646
[57] Ibid., 652

in the light becomes possible and the necessity of struggle and suffering ceases: this is for Sri Aurobindo the *deus explicitus,* in the terminology used above by J. Hirschberger: the Divine is no longer slumbering, but fully awakened and inspiring an illumined and harmonious life on earth – the life divine.

G.W.F. Hegel
with students in Berlin

6

Hegel and the Absolute Idealism

The true is the whole. But the whole is merely the essential nature reaching its completeness through the process of its own development. Of the Absolute it is to be said that it is essentially a result, that only at the end it is what it is in truth.[1]

It is the goal of world history that the spirit attains the knowledge of what it truly is and makes this knowledge concrete, realizes it in the form of an existing world, brings forth itself objectively.[2]

Humans only know of God insofar as God in humans knows of himself; this knowledge is the self-awareness of God.[3]

G.W.F. Hegel[4]

Possession in oneness and not loss in oneness is the secret. God and Man, World and Beyond-world become one when they know each other.[5]

Mind also has its own types of perfection and its absolutes. What intrusion of Overmind or Supermind could produce philosophies more perfect in themselves than the systems of Shankara or Plato or Plotinus or Spinoza or Hegel.[6]

Sri Aurobindo

---

[1] *Phänomenologie des Geistes,* Vorrede (1841), Hoffmeister, p. 21
[2] *Vorlesungen über die Philosophie der Weltgeschichte,* Einleitung (1830/31), Hoffmeister, p.74
[3] Quoted in: J. Hirschberger, *Geschichte der Philosophie,* II, 419
[4] The name is pronounced as *hegil* would be pronounced by a Hindi speaker (with a short *i*).
[5] *Essays in Philosophy and Yoga,* 202
[6] *Letters on Poetry and Art,* 72

Sri Aurobindo once referred to the question whether he was influenced by Greek or other Western philosophy. In his statement he clarified that he did read one or the other Greek author, but there were definitely not any regular studies of metaphysics at school or college:

> What little I knew about philosophy I picked up desultorily in my general reading. I once read, not Hegel, but a small book on Hegel, but it left no impression on me... German metaphysics and most European philosophy since the Greeks seemed to me a mass of abstractions with nothing concrete or real that could be firmly grasped and written in a metaphysical jargon to which I had not the key. I tried once a translation of Kant but dropped it after the first two pages and never tried again.[7]

However, as his yoga practice advanced, he developed the capacity of expressing inner experiences in an elevated philosophical language and also to evaluate the ideas of other thinkers – without significant studies of their writings – by assessing them as it were through his seer vision on the basis of some main thoughts known to him. We get a clue for this uncommon procedure in one of his texts originally written in Bengali:

> The poets of the Rigveda, the Rishis, expressed spiritual knowledge in divinely inspired words and rhythms; the Rishis of the Upanishads had direct vision of the true form of that Knowledge and expressed it in a few profound words. Not only Monism, but all the philosophical thoughts and doctrines that have come into being in Europe and Asia – Rationalism, Realism, Nihilism, the Darwinian theory of evolution, the Positivism of Comte, the philosophy of Hegel, Kant, Spinoza and Schopenhauer, Utilitarianism, Hedonism, all were seen and expressed by the Rishis endowed with the direct vision.[8]

This quotation confirms once more what we had already stated at an-

---

[7] *Autobiographical Notes*, 112
[8] sriaurobindoashram.info / Writings in Bengali Translation / The Upanishads 57

other place in connection with Neo-Platonism and its closeness to thoughts of the Upanishads: for Sri Aurobindo there exists a kind of kingdom of philosophical ideas which intuitive thinkers may access independent of time and space, receiving streams of thought from there. This also explains how it could happen – as we shall see later – that Teilhard de Chardin or Jean Gebser were able to receive certain similar ideas nearly parallel to Sri Aurobindo without initially being familiar with his works. Likewise, we may state: if Sri Aurobindo wrote some texts that were similar to those of Schelling or Hegel, it does not necessarily imply that he was drawing on the latter – it might be possible as well that he had independently developed kindred thoughts. However, we believe that the specific Noosphere in which he grew up has influenced his writing at least indirectly from the background. He has expressed thoughts for which other philosophers prepared the ground as a basic precondition for their acceptance. In a world in which for instance the term "evolution" would have been totally unknown, his whole approach may have hardly had any chance from the outset.

The philosophy of "aufheben"

There is an English word which Sri Aurobindo has used only once in his comprehensive Complete Works: it is the verb *to sublate*, which translates into German as *aufheben*, specially used by Hegel. It has four meanings, namely to lift up, to preserve and to cancel, plus a more specific philosophical meaning: a lower statement is "sublated", that is to say integrated, in a higher one. The following example may illustrate this.

Three persons see someone far away at a distance. The first says, "it is a man" (thesis), the second says, "it is a woman" (antithesis), and the third says, "it is a human being" (synthesis). So the statement "human being" does not negate the two previous statements, but rather unites them on a higher level. This implies that on the one hand they cease existing as such, but on the other hand they persist in the superordinate term. However, what Hegel has in mind is more than merely finding an umbrella term, he speaks of a "dialectical" development which effects progress in history.

In the history of philosophy, we could give the following example: Descartes presents the thesis of rationalism, which Hume confronts with the antithesis of empiricism. Then Kant reacts with the synthesis of his criticism, by discarding some elements of both of them, as he considers them erroneous, while preserving others by recognizing them as true. Thus, a new philosophy develops on a higher level in which the previous systems are "sublated". But the new thesis too is soon challenged by an antithesis negating it, which stimulates the further process of development. At the end there is Hegel's philosophy which claims to proclaim as it were the ultimate truth, with the Absolute finding itself and the dialectical process achieving completion. In this way, for Hegel his own thought is the summit and end of all philosophy, which naturally prompted others to criticize him – with the result that philosophy did not remain at a presumable final summit, but reached new heights and depths in spite of Hegel's dictum.

Although this model of thesis – antithesis – synthesis is often named after Hegel, he himself rarely used that specific formulation, but ascribed it to Kant, and it was later elaborated and popularized by Fichte. Hegel himself preferred the similar formula "abstract – negative – concrete". For him, "the concrete, the synthesis, the absolute must always pass through the phase of the negative, in the journey to completion."[9]

To return to the verb *to sublate*: Sri Aurobindo uses it once in *The Life Divine,* where an attentive disciple noticed it and asked Sri Aurobindo about its meaning.[10] In the respective passage Sri Aurobindo has written with reference to a certain type of realization: "It claims to stand behind and supersede, to sublate and to eliminate every other knowledge..." There follows an exchange about the precise meaning of the word with the disciple who finally looks it up in the *Oxford English Dictionary* where it is said that the German *aufheben* means at the same time "to destroy" and "to preserve", which Sri Aurobindo refuses to accept. He then proceeds to interpret a text of Hegel given in the *Dictionary* to illustrate the meaning of "sublate" or "*aufheben*". In the following we first render the text (which is taken from Hegel's

---

[9] See Wikipedia, "Hegelian dialectic".
[10] See *Letters on Himself and the Ashram*, 157

Logic), followed by Sri Aurobindo's commentary:

> Being passes over into Nothing, but Nothing is equally the contrary of itself, a passing over into Being, Coming-to-be. This Coming-to-be is the other direction; Nothing passes over into Being, but Being equally sublates itself, and is a passing over into Nothing, Ceasing-to-be. They sublate not themselves antagonistically, not the one the other externally; but each sublates itself in itself, and is in its own self the contrary of itself.

*

> Being passes over into Non-being, so it sublates itself, changes and eliminates itself as it were from the view, becomes Non-being instead of being; but so also does Non-being; what was Non-being passes over into being; where there was nothing, there is being; nothing has eliminated itself from the view. This, says Hegel, is not a mutual destruction by two contraries each of which was outside the other... They do not really sublate or drive out each other, but each sublates itself into the other. In other words, it is the same Reality that presents itself now as one and now as the other.[11]

It is interesting to compare Sri Aurobindo's explications with the following note on "Aufheben" in the English Wikipedia, which confirms his rejection of the Dictionary's meaning "preserve and destroy": "Sublation can be seen at work at the most basic level of Hegel's system of logic. The two concepts *Being* and *Nothing* are each both *preserved* and *changed* through sublation in the concept of Becoming." So we may note that Sri Aurobindo, although he has no direct knowledge of the philosophical meaning of *aufheben*, is able to explore the text through intuition, revealing its central statement.

Critique of dialectical reasoning

In a chapter titled "The Eternal and the Individual" in *The Life Divine* Sri Aurobindo raises the topic of mental logic and its limits and also

---

[11] Ibid.

refers to dialectics.[12] The latter term has existed since the epoch of Greek philosophy as an art of reasoning and science of logic, but is especially associated with Hegel. In his writing titled *The Encylopedia of Sciences* he defines it as "the scientific application of the patterns inherent in the nature of thinking and at the same time this law itself". G. Schischkoff explains Hegel's dialectics more concretely as "the movement which underlies everything as truly spiritual[13] reality and simultaneously that of human thinking which as speculation has an all-comprehensive, absolute share in this movement... The law of the moving thought is that of the moving world."[14]

Sri Aurobindo states in the above-mentioned chapter that it might be difficult to comprehend some of his concepts with the normal logical reason and proposes to meet this difficulty with the help of a "larger and more catholic enlightening reason". Then he continues,

> Or if it is a difficulty of spiritual experience, it can only be met by a wider resolving experience. It can indeed be met also by a dialectical battle, a logomachy of the logical mind, but that by itself is an artificial method, often a futile combat in the clouds and always inconclusive.[15]

Sri Aurobindo continues pointing out that logical thought is certainly useful and indispensable in its own field, for it gives clarity and precision to the mind in dealing with its own ideas. Thus, what we have achieved physically, psychologically or spiritually, "may be as little as possible obscured by the confusions of our average human intelligence."

> That clarification, the habit of clear logical reasoning culminating in the method of metaphysical dialectics, does help to accomplish and its part in the preparation of knowledge is therefore very great. But by itself it cannot arrive either at the knowledge of the world or the knowledge of God, much less reconcile the lower and the higher reali-

---

[12] *The Life Divine*, 381f
[13] geistig.
[14] *Philosophisches Wörterbuch*, Stuttgart 1978, p. 126
[15] *The Life Divine*, 381

sation. It is much more efficiently a guardian against error than a discoverer of truth, - although by deduction from knowledge already acquired it may happen upon new truths and indicate them for experience or for the higher and larger truth-seeing faculties to confirm.[16]

Thus, Sri Aurobindo makes it clear that for him the spiritual knowledge, the inner *vision* of the truth is the last word, but he also rates relatively highly the intelligent logical thinking.

Hegel's philosophy

Several articles have been published on Sri Aurobindo and Hegel. In this present chapter we will present two important studies of the professors of philosophy S.K. Maitra and Steve Odin, with the latter knowing the article of the first.[17] Both of them treat the subject in great detail, but with different focal points. Moreover, Maitra openly presents himself as a keen advocate of Sri Aurobindo's philosophy, whereas Odin has written his comparative article with the neutrality that is required for an academic journal, which does not exclude that in the final analysis he too has sympathies for Sri Aurobindo. But before discussing these two articles, we will have a brief look at a few aspects of Hegel's philosophy in order to create a background for the following exposition.

Hegel's thought has a reputation for being very difficult or even inaccessible, which, however, is not seen as a negative point by some observers, but is rather interpreted as an indication of its high quality. The American scholar Will Durant notes with some amusement that Hegel's title *Logic* "captivated Germany by its unintelligibility, and won him the chair of philosophy at Heidelberg."[18] Of Goethe too it has been reported that he found Hegel somewhat inaccessible, though he liked him very much as a fellow human and as an inspiring dialogue partner. And furthermore, the poet Heinrich Heine has reported:

---

[16] Ibid., 382
[17] S.K. Maitra, *The Meeting of the East and the West in Sri Aurobindo's Philosophy*. Sri Aurobindo and Hegel, Pondicherry 1968, pp. 170ff; Steve Odin, *Sri Aurobindo and Hegel on the Involution-Evolution of Absolute Spirit*. Philosophy East and West, Vol. 31, No. 2 (Apr. 1981), pp. 179-191. Also published in: P. Heehs, *Situating Sri Aurobindo*, 181ff
[18] *The Story of Philosophy,* New York 1961, 16

"When Hegel was dying, he said: 'Just a single person has understood me', but at once added with a sullen face: 'And even he hasn't understood me either.'"[19]

However, Sri Aurobindo's *The Life Divine* too is a closed book to many readers. There is a significant difference, though, because Sri Aurobindo's key statements can be translated into relatively simple language, and his spiritual collaborator, the Mother, has occasionally done this, as has been shown in the previous chapter. Moreover, Sri Aurobindo himself has also clarified many points in his letters and talks.

Fichte and Schelling had established the subjective and objective idealism respectively. Georg Wilhelm Friedrich Hegel (1770-1831) had the intention to take their philosophies, which from his viewpoint still had some shortcomings, to a higher and final stage with his absolute idealism. His thought was meant to be scientific and systematic, comprehending "all that is". His most well-known and influential work, the *Phenomenology of the Spirit*, completed in 1806, aims at exploring the different forms of manifestation of the spirit. Later works of Hegel are essentially considered to be further elaborations of this book.

The knowledge of truth appears to him possible only through viewing the world and the cosmos as a whole, not as something static, but rather as something that is becoming. In his preface he states: "The true is the whole. But the whole is merely the essential nature reaching its completeness[20] through the process of its own development." The Absolute is essentially *result* and only *at the end* what it is in truth. It is the function of philosophy to reveal this process of development, un-folding. But while Sri Aurobindo's aim was to have some influence on humans and the world through his writings by means of highly inspired thoughts for the sake of progressive evolution, Hegel declared that it was not the mission of philosophy to make the reality, but to know and describe it as given. Nevertheless, his thought became a powerful factor in world history in spite of this theoretical determination, because Karl Marx adopted some of his approaches

---

[19] *Aphorismen.de* - Zitate
[20] Or, perfection.

(with modifications), especially the method of dialectics.

In his *Encyclopedia of Philosophical Sciences* (1817) Hegel delineates the different stages of development and forms of manifestation of the spirit. The latter becomes its own object in its various forms of manifestation; it is like humans watching their own image in a mirror. There is the *subjective* spirit, existing in the shape of reason and self-awareness in individuals, as well as the *objective* spirit, reflected in the social world of economy, law and state, and finally the *absolute* spirit as summit of all development, with its three forms of viewing, visualizing and knowing.[21] The stage of viewing is found in art, where the ideal shines through matter as it were; in religion there is visualization in the form of a transcendent person, that is, God. And finally, in philosophy emerges the reason-based science of knowledge and the Absolute becomes aware of itself as eternal Idea and Creator of Nature. In it all opposites are sublated and reconciled with each other.

This is only a very brief summary of some of the key ideas of Hegel's thought. It is important to know that for him the world is permanently in a process of becoming, as is also the case with Heraclitus, and that conflict "is the father of all things". With the spirit unfolding in matter, opposites and conflicts arise, causing movement and vitality. But inherent in this process there is a striving for union and harmonization. In this context Hegel uses the word *aufheben*, to sublate: thesis and antithesis (or the abstract − negative) as the two poles are sublated in a synthesis, which is not to be understood as a kind of compromise, but rather as a movement from inner contradictions to a high-level integration or unification, with the essence of the respective truths remaining preserved.

World-spirit and world-history

Hegel's rather difficult philosophy becomes more accessible when we are dealing with the above-mentioned *objective* spirit, the working of the *Weltgeist* in world-history, which however from his viewpoint reduces itself largely to European history. He believes that history is interwoven with the principle of reason; it is not a sequence of futile

---

[21] Anschauung, Vorstellen, Erkennen.

events, but a dialectically unfolding development in which reason is steadily gaining more and more ground. He also defines world history as "progress in the consciousness of freedom" and points out concretely that in the ancient Orient, that is Egypt and Persia, only a single person was free, namely the ruler; in the Greek and Roman world a few (aristocrats), whereas only in the modern Christian world freedom is achieved by the community.

Great historical figures such as Caesar or Napoleon unknowingly place themselves in the service of the world-spirit, which realizes its objectives with their help, thus advancing the progress of history. They initiate new epochs through their actions, but fail if they try to stay on the stage beyond their appointed time, after their purpose has been fulfilled. Violent conflicts take place in the theatre of world-history, stimulating its advancement; "it is not the ground of happiness," as he once said in a lecture on the philosophy of history. Periods of happiness are for him "empty pages", for they are periods of "lacking opposites".[22]

Nevertheless, there is – as in philosophy – in politics too a stage of perfection. In the latter there ends the historical need of conflict and violence, with the world-spirit perfectly finding itself in a highest form of state. This Hegel identified with the constitutional monarchy of the Prussian State, in whose services he was a professor of philosophy. Problematic and often criticized is his maxim, "what is reasonable is real, and what is real is reasonable,"[23] for naturally this can serve as a justification for any authoritarian form of government, even of the worst kind. Certainly, it would be wrong to interpret this statement superficially and one-sidedly; we have to consider the possibility of a deeper dimension of its content. Thus, the Hegel expert Hermann Glockner points out that it does not refer directly to the Prussian State and nor to the transient historical moment, "but to that 'eternal present' which is 'always there' and contains, sublated in it, all the past."[24] However, it is a fact that the Prussian government made Hegel's philosophy the foundation of its concept of the state.

It is characteristic of Hegel's vision of world history that individu-

---

[22] See Wiedmann, *Hegel*, 82
[23] Quoted from the Preface of *Grundlinien der Philosophie des Rechts*.
[24] Quoted in Wiedmann, *Hegel*, 79

als take a back seat, "their freedom consists only in the destruction of the arbitrary isolation and their integration into a general moral Whole."²⁵ Even the above-mentioned great historical figures are in his eyes only "chief executives of the world-spirit", the "ruse of reason" uses them for its special purposes. In a final quotation of Hegel on this subject there is an equation of history-shaping reason and divine providence, and once more we come across the term *Nous*:

> The truth, then, that a divine Providence (that of God) presides over the events of the world, consorts with the proposition in question. For the divine Providence is Wisdom, endowed with an infinite Power which realizes its aim, viz. the absolute rational final design of the world; reason is thought determining itself with perfect freedom, *Nus*.²⁶

S.K. Maitra's critique of Hegel

Johannes Hirschberger describes Hegel's idealism as "typical philosophy of becoming": "The Absolute requires the becoming to find itself and therefore enters the path of continuous development."²⁷ This latter term is exactly the point where Maitra starts with his Hegel-critique. For him development with Hegel is an evolution according to plan, on given mental tracks as it were. Several times he uses the word "block universe", a difficult technical term which basically stands for the conception that all events of the future are set in the same way as those of the past and present, that is to say a kind of determinism.

As the deeper cause for this defect, as he sees it, Maitra makes out Hegel's equation of Thought and Being:

> What, however, is his conception of the nature of Thought? What is for him the essential feature of the World-view of Thought? Expressed in one word, it is: Continuity. The world of thought knows no gaps anywhere. As thought and reality are identical for him, this means also

---

²⁵ Ibid., 82
²⁶ Hegel quoted in: K. Rossmann, *Deutsche Geschichtsphilosophie*, München 1960, p. 243
²⁷ *Geschichte der Philosophie*, II, 412

that reality has no gaps or discontinuities anywhere.[28]

After some more explanations Maitra addresses the subject of evolutionary theories and states that in our contemporary discourse we should especially focus on the question of opting for the model of either a continuous or an emergent evolution. The first he describes "as a very tame affair, compared with that based on the principle of emergence. Its dance is a marionette dance, not at all comparable to the world-shaking and world-shaping dance of Shiva which is envisaged by emergent evolution. Its chief defect is its self-centered isolation; it cuts us off from the spiritual forces which are but dimly perceived by us... It must realize that the course of the world is not something that can be calculated beforehand... Continuity can function very well in a ready-made world, but it can give no guidance in a world which is constantly springing surprises upon us."[29]

But Maitra has a deep knowledge of Hegel's philosophy and can easily guess the objections of Hegelians against his theses: "They will swear that theirs is no block universe, but one which is capable of infinite expansion."[30] With reference to this issue F. Wiedmann writes in his biography of Hegel that the latter's philosophy – other than for example that of his predecessors from Descartes up to Fichte – is not to be understood, according to his own conviction, as a stage of development but as the perfect completion of history, unifying and sublating in itself all previous knowledge. "Hegel believes that after him there will be further advance, but no further ascent any more, comparable to walking on a plateau."[31]

For Maitra, this is exactly the decisive point where Hegel differs from Sri Aurobindo and his vision of the future: as in the past the principles of matter, life, mind, and soul have emerged, so more of them (like supermind) await humans in the future evolution, effecting a fundamental change of their life. Maitra then figures out what Sri Aurobindo would tell the Hegelians: "No doubt you have worked wonders with the help of the few principles that were at your disposal,

---

[28] Maitra, *The Meeting of the East and the West in Sri Aurobindo's Philosophy*, 176
[29] Ibid., 185-86
[30] Ibid. 186
[31] F. Wiedmann, *Hegel*, Reinbek 2010, pp.82-83

but for God's sake, do not mortgage the future, for it is replete with possibilities, of which you cannot form the faintest idea."[32]

With reference to Maitra's comparative study we may note critically, though, that he contrasts Hegel's "continuous" and Sri Aurobindo's "emergent" evolution without mentioning that Sri Aurobindo himself uses the term "continuity" in connection with his own model. In fact, this is not a contradiction, for in his concept this term stands for the steady, persistent working of a higher, not in any way limiting law, namely that of the complex process of evolution, with the significant feature of emergence. The following passage from *The Life Divine* will illustrate this point. In a chapter titled "Ascent and Integration" he writes:

> To each grade in this series[33] achieved by the evolving Consciousness belongs its appropriate class of existences, - one by one there appear material forms and forces, vegetable life, animals and half-animal man, developed human beings, imperfectly evolved or more evolved spiritual beings: but because of the *continuity*[34] of the evolutionary process there is no rigid separation between them; each new advance or formation takes up what was before...
>
> The evolving Consciousness passes from one grade to another or from one series of steps to another either by an imperceptible process or by some bound or crisis or, perhaps, by an intervention from above, – some descent or ensouling or influence from higher planes of Nature.
>
> Thus has come about the present status of the evolution of which man is the now apparent culmination but not the real ultimate summit; for he is himself a transitional being and stands at the turning-point of the whole movement. Evolution, being thus *continuous*, must have at any given moment a past with its fundamental results still in evidence, a present in which the results it is labouring over are in process of becoming, a future in which still unevolved powers and forms of being must appear till there is the full and perfect manifestation.[35]

---

[32] *Maitra*, 186
[33] Series of matter, life, mind etc.
[34] Italics, W.H.
[35] *The Life Divine*, 735

Steve Odin's comparative study

The approach of Odin's treatise is quite different from that of S.K. Maitra. While the latter seems to be more intent on analysing differences (as was also the case in his study of Plato), Odin focusses more on common points and even insinuates that Sri Aurobindo has adopted key ideas from Hegel. Thus, he says for example:

> The twentieth-century Indian philosopher Sri Aurobindo, who has framed his own full-scale metaphysical synthesis, appropriated Hegel's notion of an Absolute Spirit and employed it to radically restructure the architectonic framework of the ancient Hindu Vedānta system in contemporary terms.[36]

Even during his life-time Sri Aurobindo was confronted with similar views. In a talk dated 26 August 1940 he comments on C.C. Dutt's review of his work *The Life Divine* and refers to Dutt's statement that he has "derived his technique from Shankara" (it is not quite obvious what Dutt wants to suggest here). Sri Aurobindo clarifies, "That is not true. I have not read much of philosophy. It is like those who say that I am influenced by Hegel."[37] In another talk he explains: "People think I must be immensely learned and know all about Hegel, Kant and the others. The fact is that I haven't even read them; and people don't know I have written everything from experience and spiritual perception."[38] Nevertheless, even the well-versed Sri Aurobindo expert S.K. Maitra writes in his comparative study:

> [Sri Aurobindo] is not in the habit of mentioning names, but as one reads his books, one cannot fail to notice how thorough is his grasp of the great Western philosophers of the present age, such as Kant, Hegel, Spencer and Bergson. He is also very well acquainted with the latest developments of scientific thought in the West.
> When I say, therefore, that Sri Aurobindo belongs to our *āryabhūmi*,[39]

---

[36] *Steve Odin*, 179
[37] Purani, *Evening Talks*, 106
[38] Nirodbaran, *Talks with Sri Aurobindo*, 5-3-1940
[39] Our Indian country. (W.H.)

the last thing which I have in mind is to underrate the influence of Western thought upon him. That influence is there, very clearly visible, but Sri Aurobindo, a great creative genius as he is, has not allowed himself to be dominated by it. He has made full use of Western thought, but he has made use of it for the purpose of building up his own system which he has reared upon the solid foundations of our own culture with which he has a very direct and intimate contact through original sources.[40]

With these remarks, Maitra seems to go far beyond what Sri Aurobindo himself concedes in his own statements, and Odin again goes a step further with his assertion that Sri Aurobindo has adopted a key idea directly from Hegel. However, we believe that Odin does not intend to criticize Sri Aurobindo through this pronouncement, for in the history of philosophy transfers of ideas are quite common. What really matters is the creativity of the philosopher, his art of filling an idea with life and significant content in his own system.

In what follows only some central points of Odin's long article will be referred to. At the beginning he discusses especially Hegel's and Sri Aurobindo's concept of the Absolute and concludes that Hegel sees the Absolute as "dialectical idea", whereas Sri Aurobindo formulates it "in terms of a radiant and ecstatic supramental awareness, Existence-Consciousness-Bliss", called Sachchidananda in Vedanta. Yet Sri Aurobindo has adopted, claims Odin, "the essential structure of Hegel's concept of the Absolute, which is precisely the Absolute as living 'Spirit'."[41] Next Odin explains the concept of Spirit projected outward and objectified as material nature, and in the end finding itself through a dialectical process of development and returning to itself as the eternal Absolute.

Thus, the Being of the Absolute cannot be thought of as something inert and static, "but must rather be conceived as a self-revealing, self-manifesting consciousness... World creation, therefore, is not something arbitrary but something belonging to the very structure of God. Yet the Absolute is not only to be grasped as an eternal creator, as

---

[40] *Maitra*, 49
[41] *Steve Odin*, 181

passing outside itself, but also a real evolution and return to self."
Odin then quotes Hegel with the following words:

> If God is defined merely as the Creator, His activity is taken only as going outside of itself as a material producing, without any return into itself. God is indeed more than this. He is... the mediation of Himself with Himself.[42]

Odin comments that this is a brilliant aspect of Hegel's philosophy, this projecting outward into otherness, in which He reflects himself, rediscovers and reunites himself. Through this process the Absolute does not remain merely an abstract substance, but becomes concretely a subject. Odin adds another quotation from Hegel which he considers to be one of his best inspired utterances:

> To know what God as spirit is – to apprehend this accurately and distinctly in thoughts – requires careful and thorough speculation. It includes, in its forefront the propositions: God is God only so far as he knows himself: his self-knowledge is further, a self-consciousness in man and man's knowledge *of* God, which proceeds to man's self-knowledge *in* God.[43]

Once more Odin asserts that Sri Aurobindo has built on these thoughts of Hegel, restructuring the architectonic scaffolding of the ancient Vedanta system into evolutionary terms with the notion of a dynamic activity of the Absolute in the form of self-differentiation and reconciliation. Furthermore, Odin points out that in Sri Aurobindo's "Neo-Vedantic ontology" there is a concept of Brahman-Shakti, with the Brahman standing for the static consciousness, whereas the Shakti, adopted from the tantric philosophy, denotes creative vitality and joyous self-manifesting power.

Next he discusses Sri Aurobindo's key idea of a Sevenfold Chord of Being, which includes the lower hemisphere of matter-life-mind, the higher of Sat-Chit-Ananda, and as an intermediary principle su-

---

[42] Ibid., 182
[43] Ibid., 183

permind. He adds a very well-chosen quotation from *The Life Divine*:

> The Divine descends from pure existence through the play of Consciousness-Force and Bliss and the creative medium of Supermind into cosmic being; we ascend from Matter through a developing life, soul and mind and the illuminating medium of Supermind towards the divine being. The knot of the two, the higher and the lower hemisphere, is where mind and supermind meet with a veil between them.[44]

Odin points out that this concept differs significantly from Shankara's illusionism insofar as the creation is seen as fully real and ultimately the field of the divine manifestation, the divine Ananda, bliss. He also mentions a quotation from the Taittiriya Upanishad in Sri Aurobindo's translation: "From Delight all these beings are born, by Delight they exist and grow, to Delight they return."[45] After some more deliberations Odin undertakes a comparison with Hegel's concept of development, and comments:

> At this point certain aspects of Sri Aurobindo's evolutionary scheme should be considered in its relation to Hegel's. Both philosophers similarly envision world creation as the progressive self-manifestation and evolutionary ascent of a universal consciousness in its journey toward self-realization. Yet, as opposed to the deterministic and continuous dialectical unfolding of Absolute Reason by the mechanism of thesis-antithesis-synthesis, or affirmation-negation-integration, Sri Aurobindo argues for a creative, emergent mode of evolution. Unlike the Hegelian scheme, involution-evolution or creation and return are not necessary moments of Spirit determined strictly by its intrinsic logical structure; nor is the course of evolution itself a mechanistic unfolding of a pre-existent logical pattern. Rather, involution-evolution occurs only due to the cosmic *līlā*, that is, the creative play or spontaneous self-expressiveness emerging from the plenary delight of Brahman-Shakti.[46]

---

[44] *The Life Divine*, 278. Odin's text contains some minor modifications; we have given the original text.
[45] *The Life Divine*, 98
[46] *Steve Odin*, 186

In his résumé Odin finally arrives at the conclusion that Sri Aurobindo has overcome, by incorporating a historical and evolutionary perspective in his philosophy, "the greatest shortcoming of traditional Hindu thought", namely its ahistorical world-vision and "its utter disengagement from the richness of social-technological life." At the same time he has avoided Hegel's deterministic evolutionism by presenting a concept "which allows for a genuine creative advance and emergent novelty in the self-unfolding of living Spirit."[47]

Next Odin states that Sri Aurobindo's concept, by including an involution, has a definite explanatory advantage over kindred doctrines of contemporary philosophers such as Bergson or Whitehead, whose evolutionary schemes do not satisfactorily explain the purpose of it all. Hegel, he says, was the first to clearly articulate the involutional-evolutional structure of reality, but he too failed to provide an explanation concerning the purpose of the cosmological process, as he offered only "an epistemological explanation based on the necessity for self-reflection in the course of Spirit's coming to knowledge of itself." In contrast, Sri Aurobindo bases his concept of involution-evolution ultimately in Ananda, the divine delight of a free, cosmic self-unfolding, not conditioned by any inherent necessity and therefore more in agreement with the concept of an "Absolute".

Furthermore, says Odin, Sri Aurobindo has united the personal and transpersonal domains of experience in his teaching of "integral transformation", and it is only this kind of life-affirming, value-centric vision of reality, acknowledging its static as well as dynamic poles, that can be helpful in achieving spiritual perfection in the complexity of modern technological society. Thus, due to its comprehensiveness, Sri Aurobindo's world hypothesis "has performed the great service of reinstating Absolute Idealism as a plausible philosophical alternative in the contemporary world."[48]

Sri Aurobindo's philosophy of history

During his schooldays in England Sri Aurobindo was keenly interest-

---

[47] *Steve Odin*, 190
[48] Ibid.

ed in historical subjects and acquired a solid knowledge of world history. He knew Hegel's term *Weltgeist* and occasionally uses the English equivalent "world-spirit" in his writings. Thus, in 1910 he notes in his essay *The Ideal of the Karmayogin*:

> The world moves through an indispensable interregnum of free thought and materialism to a new synthesis of religious thought and experience, a new religious world-life free from intolerance, yet full of faith and fervour, accepting all forms of religion because it has an unshakable faith in the One. The religion which embraces Science and faith, Theism, Christianity, Mahomedanism and Buddhism and yet is none of these, is that to which the World-Spirit moves.[49]

At another place he mentions, in a certain context, "the world-spirit having greater ends before it and a greater law to realise."[50] Such statements are characteristic of his view of history, for it is his basic assumption – in tune with his theory of evolution – that history develops progressively, though not in a linear, but spiral form. There are times of great progress, then setbacks, decadence, and finally new impulses and a gradual acquiring and stabilizing of achievements.

For Sri Aurobindo, the true values of life are clearly defined through his spiritual philosophy. The supramental consciousness stands for unity, freedom, harmony, love in their spiritual form of expression. In the relative world they are the *divine* forces, which are confronted with the *asuric* such as division, suppression, hatred, cruelty. Based on these criteria, even after his retreat from politics in 1910 Sri Aurobindo had an eye on current developments in the world. For his integral yoga has been conceived as a collective yoga, which means that the ideals envisaged by him are first to be realized in a small community, but ultimately in the whole world. He has especially dealt with this topic in his title *The Ideal of Human Unity*.

But he also discusses subjects of the philosophy of history in his title *The Human Cycle*. Taking up some theses of the German professor of history, Karl Lamprecht, who abandoned the traditional descrip-

---

[49] *Essays in Philosophy and Yoga*, 6
[50] Ibid. 410

tive method and tried to discover patterns that underlie the growth of nations, Sri Aurobindo develops his own theory and presents the vision of history unfolding in certain stages with their respective own characteristics. The present "subjective age", he believes, will merge into a spiritual or even supramental age in which humans are guided by a divine Light in whatever they think and do.

Although Sri Aurobindo did study social life, too, there is no doubt that – in comparison with other thinkers like Hegel – he was focussing more on the development of individuals. Accordingly, Sushmita Bhowmik correctly states in an article on "Sri Aurobindo and the Uplift of Humanity":

> Although the total aim of Sri Aurobindo has always been the perfection not only of the individual but also of the society and eventually of the whole of humanity, it might be pointed out that in his thoughts and writings there is a greater primary emphasis on individual perfection than on social perfection. But here it has to be noted that, since according to Sri Aurobindo individual is the key of the evolutionary movement, he has had to focus his attention initially to a greater degree on the problem of individual perfection than on social perfection.[51]

Sri Aurobindo never was under the illusion that a mere outer change of system could effect a great change for the world. Certainly, a proper external frame of life is necessary in which humans are able to follow their personal vocation in freedom and self-determination. He always thought this to be very important and therefore worked intensively for the Indian independence movement after his return from England. But even in a democracy every state is only as good as the humans who constitute it, and every lasting progress must therefore start with the individuals and aim at encouraging the true values and spiritual inclinations in them. Thus, he writes in an aphorism:

> This erring race of human beings dreams always of perfecting their environment by the machinery of government and society; but it is on-

---

[51] Sanyal and Roy, *Understanding Thoughts of Sri Aurobindo*, 219

ly by the perfection of the soul within that the outer environment can be perfected. What thou art within, that outside thee thou shalt enjoy; no machinery can rescue thee from the law of thy being.[52]

Sri Aurobindo's ideas of future political developments, world union and harmony are often felt to be utopian by outsiders. However, he was also a realist and has envisaged these perspectives as very long-term possibilities. We believe that from his viewpoint humanity would already have covered a decisive stage if standards of the European Union, for instance, in international relations would be world-wide established, with the corresponding human rights and a culture of diplomacy in dealing with conflicts. Sri Aurobindo has expressed his high opinion of Europe on several occasions, also in a letter to his brother Barin in 1920, in which he states that in Europe there is a great culture of thinking and striving for knowledge.[53] Furthermore, he has mentioned the idea of European unity in his title *The Ideal of Human Unity* and endorsed it on condition that it does not go along with the suppression of other continents. However, his ultimate and highest perspective was not European, but global – the idea of unity for the whole world.

---

[52] *Essays Dvine and Human*, 468
[53] See W. Huchzermeyer, *Sri Aurobindo*, Saga of a Great Indian Sage, p. 193

F. Nietzsche

7

Nietzsche and the Ideal of Superman

But actually we do not want to enter into the kingdom of heaven: we have become men, so we want the kingdom of earth.
... *the heart of the earth is of gold.*[1]

F. Nietzsche

I am concerned with the earth and not with worlds beyond for their own sake; it is a terrestrial realisation that I seek and not a flight to distant summits.[2]

Sri Aurobindo

Nietzsche's superman is very like Siegfried, except that he knows Greek.[3]

Bertrand Russell

Nietzsche hymned the Olympian, but presented him with the aspect of the Asura.[4]

Sri Aurobindo

Sri Aurobindo has referred very frequently to Nietzsche[5] (1844-1900) in his writings, we have compiled in total 28 quotations in a German comparative study on Nietzsche and Sri Aurobindo.[6] Their content will be summarized in the following.

It is the great merit of Nietzsche that he reintroduced dynamism

---

[1] *Thus spoke Zarathustra*, chapter 90, The Donkey Festival; chapter 51, Great Events.
[2] *Letters on Yoga II*, 482
[3] *A History of Western Philosophy*, 760. Siegfried is one of the heroes of the German *Nibelungen saga*.
[4] *Essays in Philosophy and Yoga*, The Superman, 152
[5] His name is pronounced like Sanskrit *nīce*.
[6] *Der Übermensch – bei Friedrich Nietzsche und Sri Aurobindo*, Gladenbach 1986, Anhang I

and practical force into Western philosophy, that he developed intuitive vision as a means of finding the Truth. A similar role was played by H. Bergson in modern France and Heraclitus in ancient Greece. In fact, Nietzsche has much in common with the Greek mystic. Both stress the principles of war and struggle as evolutionary forces. But Nietzsche is one-sided in so far as he denies Being as the ground of Becoming. Nevertheless, among modern thinkers Nietzsche is "the most vivid, concrete and suggestive." All in all, his philosophy is stimulating, although it "solves nothing".[7]

Nietzsche was a seer by nature, at times he had extraordinary visions. Often, however, he misinterpreted his own visions or received them wrongly. One of his brilliant ideas was that of the *Übermensch* or superman, he was the first to popularize it in European thought. But though the concept of a future being of a higher species is great as such, one cannot accept its actual content. Nietzsche spoilt and mishandled his own idea because he was confused about the figures of God and Titan, or Deva and Asura in Indian terminology. Rejecting violently the idea of the suffering, crucified Christ, he presents us "the Olympian... with the aspect of the Asura", a Greek God with some titanic characteristics.[8]

But sometimes the German poet-philosopher overcomes his personal idiosyncracies and pierces straight into the heart of the Truth. At such moments he is the pure seer who has "rare gleaming intuitions" and speaks out the word as it has come "to his inner hearing vibrating out of a distant infinite like a strain caught from the lyre of far-off Gods."[9] When Nietzsche stated that we have to develop a superman out of our present unsatisfactory manhood, he was absolutely right. His idea that we have to exceed ourselves, "could not be bettered."[10] But the difficulty was that he had no clear notion of the true "Self" that is to be discovered.

The main defect of Nietzsche's superman is that he loses the link to moral evolution. Thus he becomes a figure who shuns sorrow and service and strives to dominate his environment. In this sense Nie-

---

[7] *Essays in Philosophy and Yoga*, 224
[8] Ibid. 152
[9] Ibid.
[10] *The Human Cycle*, 233

tzsche's philosophy is vitalistic. Since he has no concept of a supreme Being above, his superman with his one-sided ascent has no sense of surrender, of offering himself up into something Greater. Instead of growing spiritually, he would rather widen his ego and expand it enormously. In that respect there is a vast gap between Nietzsche's Übermensch and Sri Aurobindo's superman.

However, the two thinkers agree in their rejection of a flight from the world and of the ideal of a super ascetic: they want to focus the human consciousness on the earth, they believe in its high destiny and its fulfilment through future humans. The goal is not a kingdom of heaven beyond, but a changed life here in this world.

Superman in Sri Aurobindo's main works

The idea of superman as a future stage of evolution does not exist in the Indian tradition. There are terms such as Avatar, divine incarnation; or Mahatma, highly developed soul; furthermore Siddha Yogi, a perfected yogi with siddhis or supernatural capacities such as levitation, telepathy, knowledge of the future, in individual cases also with a body developed beyond the normal human measure, free from illness and decay. And there is the image of the Gods, revealing themselves in a radiant, immaculate, immortal body.

So if Sri Aurobindo uses the term in its specific evolutionary meaning, he obviously resorts to a word established in Europe. He openly recognizes this fact by mentioning in his essay *The Superman* that it was Nietzsche who first made this term known in the cultural history. But it plays only a very small role in Sri Aurobindo's main works. The words *superman* and *supermanhood* occur only a dozen times in *The Life Divine*, which contains more than a thousand pages, and still more rarely in *The Synthesis of Yoga* or *Savitri*. In the following we render three important quotations from the first title:

> Either man must fulfil himself by satisfying the Divine within him or he must produce out of himself a new and greater being who will be more capable of satisfying it. He must either himself become a divine

humanity or give place to Superman.[11]

If [the modern thinker] sees a vision of the Superman, it is in the figure of increased degrees of mentality or vitality; he admits no other emergence, sees nothing beyond these principles, for these have traced for us up till now our limit and circle.[12]

It is in his human nature, in all human nature, to exceed itself by conscious evolution, to climb beyond what he is. Not individuals only, but in time the race also... can have the hope... to rise beyond the imperfections of our present very undivine nature and to ascend at least to a superior humanity, to rise nearer, even if it cannot absolute reach, to a divine manhood or supermanhood. At any rate, it is the compulsion of evolutionary Nature in him to strive to develop upward, to erect the ideal, to make the endeavour.[13]

Sri Aurobindo's philosophy is marked by its firm evolutionary optimism. Glancing from Timelessness with his seer-eye, he perceives in the world of becoming the progressive impulse in creation, with the latter orienting itself towards the light like a plant. In humans the divine seed lies dormant, the archetype of the True, the Good and Beautiful, preparing its path towards unfoldment over the ages. A thousand obstacles or setbacks may come up, thick crusts may have to be pierced through, but in the end nothing can stop the evolutionary progress.

But whoever envisions a future with humans merely developing some superior vitality and higher intelligence, falls short of the real ideal, according to Sri Aurobindo's conviction. He sees, on the one hand, the possibility of spiritually transformed humans making great progress especially on the plane of consciousness. But ultimately the supreme light should also become effective on the physical plane. Therefore Sri Aurobindo considers, on the other hand, the possibility of humans giving way to superman. Here he refers to what he calls in another chapter "a supramental spiritual being who shall impose on

---

[11] *The Life Divine*, 222
[12] Ibid., 284
[13] Ibid., 745

his mental, vital, bodily workings a higher law than that of the dividing Mind." Sri Aurobindo further points out in this chapter titled "The Knot of Matter":

> Such a supramental being would, as we have seen, liberate the mind from the knot of its divided existence and use the individualisation of mind as merely a useful subordinate action of the all-embracing Supermind.

Sri Aurobindo continues that the life force too would be similarly liberated and finally voices the rather revolutionary idea that in the end there might be a break-through even on the physical plane:

> Is there any reason why he should not also liberate the bodily existence from the present law of death, division and mutual devouring... or why this spirit should not be free in a sovereign occupation of form, consciously immortal even in the changing of his robe of Matter...?[14]

Many of his statements in this field are formulated cautiously, enquiringly, as he indicates possibilities which had hardly ever before been envisaged except in the circles of some highly developed yogis. In his essay *The Supramental Manifestation* he discusses this subject of a perfect spiritualized body in still greater detail and more concretely.[15] But high ideals and visions always also go along with the scepticism or rejection of some observers. These reactions already existed at Sri Aurobindo's time, as can be seen from the following letter of a disciple, written in 1933:

> Your 'superman' reminds me of an interesting debate we had. Some people ridicule us for our aspiration after supermanhood. They say it is not a sober aspiration. We don't even have the divine realisation, and we want the supramental? I replied that it is Sri Aurobindo who wants the supermind for us.[16]

---

[14] *The Life Divine*, 264
[15] See *Essays in Philosophy and Yoga*, 536ff
[16] *Letters on Himself and the Ashram*, 282

Sri Aurobindo answered that the "divine realisation", that is to say that of the Self on the mental-spiritual or overmental plane, is easier to attain and has been achieved in the past by thousands (and is not the real challenge for himself). And further he writes: "Also nobody can have the supramental realisation who has not had the spiritual. So far your opponent is right."[17]

In another letter Sri Aurobindo declares that great aspirations are legitimate "provided one does not make too personal or egoistic an affair of it turning it into a Nietzschean or other ambition to be a superman." Actually, this is the real danger with this kind of ideal and therefore Sri Aurobindo has persistently discouraged his disciples in his correspondence whenever he sensed some inappropriate aspiration in them. Ideally, every realisation should be regarded "as the fulfilment of God's working in the world, not as a personal chance or achievement."[18] Very clear is also his response to a correspondent who raises the question whether future integral yogis could not achieve a greater realisation than even Krishna, who was an Avatar of the Overmind in Sri Aurobindo's eyes. But the latter answered: "What is all this obsession of greater or less? In our Yoga we do not strive after greatness."[19]

Finally, we would have to clarify with reference to this subject of future transformation that the development of a new body as a more transparent and plastic being for the divine spirit was a very distant perspective for Sri Aurobindo, he once spoke of a period of a few hundred years. Primarily, his objective was the growth of *consciousness* and therefore terms such as *supermind* and not *superman* are central in *The Life Divine* and *The Synthesis of Yoga*. This priority also becomes evident from the following passage of a letter to a disciple:

> The aim of the Yoga is to open the consciousness to the Divine, to live in the inner consciousness more and more while acting from it on the external life... Secondly, to develop the Yogic consciousness – i.e. to universalize the being on all the planes... Thirdly, to come into con-

---

[17] Ibid.
[18] Ibid., 283-84
[19] Ibid., 407

tact with the transcendent Divine, beyond the Overmind... and make oneself an instrument for the realisation of the dynamic Divine Truth and its transforming descent into the earth-nature.[20]

R. Safranski's portrait of Nietzsche

Rüdiger Safranski's Nietzsche study[21] is considered to be one of the best in German language. We will use his exposition in the following especially with reference to the subject of "superman" and contrast it with Sri Aurobindo's interpretations in order to get a modern parallel for the purpose of comparison and some significant key words for our investigation. We take up the reading of Safranski's biography at an advanced stage, in chapter 10. We are in the year 1881, Nietzsche stays in Sils Maria, Engadin, Switzerland. Wandering around the lake of Silvaplana, he has a great inspirational experience which he later describes in *Ecce Homo*. We had rated it as very important in our German Nietzsche title[22] and Safranski too renders it almost in full length. The following are the key statements of Nietzsche's autobiographical text:

Has anyone at the end of the 19th century any clear idea of what poets of strong ages have called *inspiration*? If not, I will describe it. If one would have the slightest trace of superstition left in oneself, it would indeed hardly be possible to reject the idea that one is merely the incarnation, mouthpiece and medium of overpowering forces. The idea of revelation, in the sense that suddenly, with unspeakable certainty and subtlety, something becomes visible, audible, something that profoundly shakes and upsets one, simply describes the fact. One hears, one does not seek; one takes and does not ask who gives; like lightening a thought flashes up with necessity, without hesitation regarding its form – I have never had any choice...
 Everything takes place involuntarily in the highest degree, but in a tempest as it were of a sense of freedom, a tempest of absoluteness,

---

[20] *Letters on Yoga II*, 20
[21] *Nietzsche – Biographie seines Denkens*. Frankfurt 2013; 1st edition München 2000. English edition: *Nietzsche – A Philosophical Biography,* trl. by S. Frisch. London 2002
[22] See *Der Übermensch* (1986), p. 10

power, divinity... The involuntariness of the figures and similes is the most noteworthy thing, you have no more any idea of what is image or simile. Everything presents itself as the closest, truest, simplest expression... This is my experience of inspiration; I do not doubt that we should have to go back thousands of years to find someone who could tell me: "It is mine also."[23]

We had already pointed out several times that the subject of "intuition" is very important for Sri Aurobindo; in this particular text and subject Nietzsche is remarkably close to him. A "strong age" would be, for the Indian seer, especially the Vedic period, when the Rishis received the mantric verses of the Rigveda with their inner hearing and sight. It continues until the epoch of the Upanishads, in which the knowledge was clothed in a more accessible language. But later the age of intuitive knowledge had to give place to the age of rational knowledge, "inspired Scripture made room for metaphysical philosophy."[24]

Perhaps the best passage in Sri Aurobindo's writings to be compared with Nietzsche's text is the following description of the phenomenon of intuition in *The Life Divine*:

> We are aware of a sealike downpour of masses of a spontaneous knowledge which assumes the nature of Thought but has a different character from the process of thought to which we are accustomed; for there is nothing here of seeking, no trace of mental construction, no labour of speculation or difficult discovery; it is an automatic and spontaneous knowledge from a Higher Mind that seems to be in possession of Truth and not in search of hidden and withheld reality.[25]

> ... The Intuition leaps out like a spark or lightening-flash...[26]

Safranski does not discuss any past ages in his further exposition, but rather describes what Nietzsche had in mind when referring to his

---

[23] *Ecce Homo*, chapter 11, section 3
[24] *The Life Divine*, 74
[25] Ibid., 291-92
[26] Ibid., 981

special experience at Silvaplana: he was receiving the idea of the Eternal Recurrence of the Same. He was so much overawed by its sublimity that he kept fluctuating between strong moods of euphoria and anxiety. And when talking about the vision to others he mostly did so in whispers only, as has also been reported by his short-term beloved, Lou Salomé. It is a real caesura in his life, he is now convinced to have a true mission, the task to proclaim a particular message. This happens at first only by way of suggestion at the end of the Fourth Book in the *Gay Science* and finally Zarathustra proclaims that thought "which needs millennia for its unfolding".

But Safranski also shows that it was not entirely new for Nietzsche, he had been dwelling on it earlier in one or the other form, taking up suggestions especially from Schopenhauer. The latter had created the image of a sun burning in the "eternal noon", while the earth is perpetually moving from day to night. Nietzsche has used the same image in *Zarathustra* in connection with the doctrine of eternal recurrence. It is worth noting that in his records he mostly gives a mathematical, mechanic meaning to this thought. Thus he speaks of a sandglass that runs out, is reversed, and will ever run out again. We may also compare this idea with a film spool being played back endlessly. Nietzsche even took up scientific studies in order to explore the law of the conservation of material substances and energies.

The idea of an eternal mechanical recurrence of the same is in a way frightening, and superman has the special capacity of not breaking under its weight. Safranski shows how Nietzsche finally took the thought to a psychological plane by pointing out that the mere idea as such of recurrence "may shatter and transform us."[27] This might be explained as follows: With the idea becoming active that every moment recurs, there is the obvious need to pay full attention to the here and now and to ask yourself, in whatever you do, "is this something that I would want to do infinite times?"

And then Nietzsche demands,

> Let us imprint the image of eternity on our life! This thought contains more than all religions which hold our present lives in contempt as be-

---

[27] Nietzsche, *Sämtliche Werke*, 9, München 1980, p. 523f.

ing ephemeral and taught us to look towards an unspecified other life.[28]

Safranski reveals how Nietzsche in this place rejects "all the ecstasies, all the bliss, all the ascensions of feeling", for what is needed is to preserve the powers of transcendence for immanence, or, in Zarathustra's words, to remain faithful to the earth – and to find bliss in the here and now. The eternal recurrence now loses its burdensome heaviness, with Nietzsche bringing in the idea of the Heraclitean cosmic game. Eternal repetition does exist, but it is joyfully experienced. Superman is the one who plays his role in the game with strength and facility. Safranski resumes: "Nietzsche's transcendence goes in the direction of regarding play as a ground of being. His Zarathustra dances when he has reached this ground; he dances like the Hindu cosmic god Shiva."[29]

In our above-mentioned German Nietzsche title we had selected some of the same quotations and stated, "Eternal recurrence is possibly a law, but in any case it can be transcended. The mechanical law itself becomes the lever to freedom and induces humans to choose a higher life."[30] And we had added an important quotation from Nietzsche:

Everything has been here before innumerable times, in so far as the total field of energy always returns. Whether, apart from this, anything identical has existed, is entirely unprovable.[31]

This thought brings Nietzsche very close to Sri Aurobindo, indeed, for the latter did not only consider reincarnation as a means for working out individual evolution, but also cyclic recurrence as a process in cosmic evolution. In the long run there is always an upward movement in spite of seeming repetition. The cosmic cycles have a hidden purpose, they return again and again until a "lesson" has been learnt and a specific constellation of forces has been mastered. In his essay

---

[28] Ibid., 9, 903
[29] *Nietzsche, Biographie seines Denkens,* 238. All quotations from this title translated by W.H.
[30] *Der Übermensch,* 49
[31] Nietzsche, *Die Unschuld des Werdens,* Band II, 463

The Hour of God Sri Aurobindo has dedicated an interesting passage to the "thought of thoughts":

> The experiment of human life on an earth is not now for the first time enacted. It has been conducted a million times before and the long drama will again a million times be repeated. In all that we do now, our dreams, our discoveries, our swift or difficult attainments we profit subconsciously by the experience of innumerable precursors and our labour will be fecund in planets unknown to us and in worlds yet uncreated. The plan, the peripeties, the denouement differ continually, yet are always governed by the conventions of an eternal Art. God, Man, nature are the three perpetual symbols.
> The idea of eternal recurrence affects with a shudder of alarm the mind entrenched in the minute, the hour, the years, the centuries, all the finite's unreal defences. But the strong soul conscious of its own immortal stuff and the inexhaustible ocean of its ever-flowing energies is seized by it with the thrill of an inconceivable rapture. It hears behind the thought the childlike laughter and ecstasy of the infinite.[32]

In his *Zarathustra* Nietzsche uses the image of a shepherd who at first suffocates in view of the prospect of having to live everything all over again in endless cycles. But then he bites off the head of this black "snake" and becomes liberated, having understood the law of recurrence which you cannot escape, but at which you can laugh, fully facing its challenge:

> No longer a shepherd, no longer a man – a transformed being, surrounded with light, and *laughing*! Never yet did any human being laugh as he did! O my brothers, I heard a laughter that was no human laughter – and now a thirst consumes me, a longing which is never stilled.[33]

Are we not actually in a position now to understand Nietzsche's inspirations with the help of Sri Aurobindo's insights? We may also com-

---

[32] *Essays Divine and Human*, 140
[33] *Zarathustra*, chapter 57, Of the Vision and the Riddle.

pare the following two passages from both thinkers, with which we conclude the subject of eternal recurrence. At first Nietzsche's text which shows that he was indeed a *poet*-philosopher:

> Everything goes, everything returns; for ever rolls the wheel of existence. Everything dies, everything blossoms anew; the year of existence runs for ever.
> Everything breaks, everything is joined anew; the same house of existence for ever builds itself. Everything departs, everything meets once more; the ring of existence is true to itself for ever.
> In every moment existence begins; the ball There rolls around every Here. The middle is everywhere. Crooked is the path of eternity.[34]

And Sri Aurobindo says:

> For when was the beginning? At no moment in Time, for the beginning is at every moment; the beginning always was, always is and always shall be. ...
> And where is the middle? There is no middle; for there is only the junction of the perpetual end and the eternal beginning; it is the sign of a creation which is new at every moment. ...
> And when is the end? There is no end. At no conceivable moment can there be a cessation. For all end of things is the beginning of new things which are still the same One in an ever developing and every recurring figure. ...[35]

We return now to Safranski who has given us another important key word with the "cosmic God Shiva", leading over to Sri Aurobindo. In a chapter titled *The Pure Existent* he reflects on Being and Becoming and concedes reality to both of them in the same way. But how do they work together, how are they connected to each other? This is recognized through a highest experience and intuition by means of which we realize that all becoming, all change is only a mode of our being and that there is something within ourselves which is not in-

---

[34] *Zarathustra*, chapter 69, The Reconvalescent
[35] *Essays Divine and Human*, 220

volved in the process of becoming. When we live in this deeper self and act out of it, it also results in a change of our lives.[36]

However, Sri Aurobindo states that stability and becoming are only "psychological representations", that is to say relative views, of the Absolute, in the same way as oneness and multitude. Basically,

> the Absolute is beyond stability and movement as it is beyond unity and multiplicity. But it takes its eternal poise in the one and the stable and whirls round itself infinitely, inconceivably, securely in the moving and multitudinous. World-existence is the ecstatic dance of Shiva which multiplies the body of the God numberlessly to the view: it leaves that white existence precisely where and what it was, ever is and ever will be; its sole absolute object is the joy of the dancing.[37]

At this point, who could claim to be able to follow easily Sri Aurobindo's vision, to integrate it with his philosophy of involution, evolution and supramental realization? This image of the ecstatic dancing Shiva in a philosophical main work seems to burst all limits – one can well imagine how the whole Western philosophical tradition would observe dumbfounded, with great amazement, this whirling appearance of the great Indian God. Only a Schelling would not be overtaxed, and a Nietzsche would probably nod approvingly, as he had proclaimed in his *Zarathustra*:

> I would only believe in a God that knows how to dance.[38]

So the circle is complete and we may return now to Safranski, who gave us the key-word "Shiva".

Zarathustra and Superman

Safranski gives a very detailed exposition of the Übermensch in *Zarathustra*. At first he points out a paradox: Zarathustra proclaims his great message at first at a market-place where people have gathered to

---

[36] See *The Life Divine*, 85
[37] Ibid.
[38] *Thus spoke Zarathustra*, chapter 7, On Reading and Writing.

watch the feats of a tightrope walker. They are certainly not church goers with the text of the Sunday sermon still resounding in their ears, but rather a sensation-seeking crowd that wants to be well-entertained. So these worldly-minded people Zarathustra addresses with his admonition not to be intoxicated by supernatural hopes, but to remain faithful to the earth. Thus, with this particular message he is altogether the wrong man at the wrong place.

But after the prologue the whole scenario changes and Zarathustra henceforth speaks "into the void", as Safranski formulates it. He believes that Nietzsche should have better left "the last humans" on the stage, in which case the teaching of the superman would have emerged in sharper contrast, as Zarathustra would have had to contend with them. Next Safranski traces the origin of the subject of Übermensch, referring to Nietzsche's *Untimely Meditations* in which he has dealt with the question of self-configuration and self-enhancement. In connection with his studies on Schopenhauer he had reflected on the discovery of the "true Self" by taking guidance from great examples. The true Self, Nietzsche wrote, "does not lie deeply hidden within you, but immeasurably high above you or at least above what you normally take to be your 'I'."[39]

Here superman is still an elevated type of man; the great evolutionary leap is not part of the concept, it is only addressed at a later stage in some passages of *Zarathustra*. There we read that man is a transitional being, looking back to his past as an ape and having superman as a prospect in the future. In Nietzsche's records from the period of *Zarathustra* there is even a rare brief quotation in which he refers to the idea of a future evolution of the body:

The goal: evolution of the whole *body* and not only the brain.[40]

However, Nietzsche does not elaborate on this thought in *Zarathustra* – fortunately, believes Safranski, for speculations on the physical shape of the future being would only result in unintentional hilarity with Nietzsche, and therefore it is good that he abstained from them.

---

[39] *Sämtliche Werke* I, 340f
[40] Ibid., 10, 506. Fragmente 4, 17 (1883)

Nietzsche had studied Darwinism intensively, taking a critical position towards it, but he was not able entirely "to extricate himself from its powerful implications", notes Safranski. The notion of development already existed in German idealism on the plane of consciousness, but was now extended even to the biological substance.

In his report on Nietzsche's examination of this subject of visions and perspectives of a higher future development Safranski finally raises the question: "If evolution has led to humans, why should it stop with humans? Why should there not be an even higher being, a superman of a higher biological type?"[41] Here we are once more very close to Sri Aurobindo, if we omit the word "biological" which he would not use, because – as already pointed out – the further physical development was not his primary objective, but only a last consequence of an evolution of consciousness.

Darwin himself did not use the term *superman*, but reflected nonetheless on possibilities of further advancement. The fact that man has risen to the very summit of the organic scale in the course of evolution, he once wrote, "may give him hope for a still higher destiny in the distant future."[42] But why then did Nietzsche keep his distance from Darwinism, "especially the scene of pamphleteering"? Safranski's answer is brief and simple: "His superman is meant to be something original and unique."[43]

In his further exposition, Safranski confirms Sri Aurobindo's statement that Nietzsche was a confused seer, for he shows that Nietzsche represented rather contradictory ideas at different stages. On the one hand he denies in *Ecce Homo* every connection with idealistic conceptions of a merely higher man, on the other hand he had developed in earlier writings precisely such thoughts and even declared in *The Birth of the Tragedy* that nobody would dare to claim "that the saint in the desert has failed to achieve the highest purpose of the cosmic will."[44] But he is primarily concerned with the type of genius, the spirited and highly creative humans. It is only in the *Gay Science*,

---

[41] *Safranski*, 271
[42] C. Darwin, *The Descent of Man*, New York 1989, p. 644
[43] *Safranski*, 272
[44] Ibid., 273

5th Book, that the type of "amoral power nature"[45] (as Safranski formulates it) appears, and with reference to this type Sri Aurobindo made the above-mentioned critical remark that Nietzsche's superman has lost the link to moral evolution.

Safranski describes Nietzsche's superman as a being to whom self-transcendence is an aspect of the will to power, namely the power over oneself. He furnishes the law of action to himself as an individual law beyond traditional morality "which restrains ordinary humans, but can only stand in the way of the superman," comments Safranski.[46] He also integrates lower impulses and pursuits into his action, but does not admit them in their crude form, rather giving them a kind of controlled expression so that the whole spectrum of a powerful vitality is preserved.

This is only a small extract from Safranski's thoughts on Nietzsche's Übermensch, rendering the most important points. In the same way as Sri Aurobindo, Safranski reveals in his critique the great variety of Nietzsche's statements, at times also contradictions, and draws our attention to dangers and deep abysses that arise as a result of certain approaches of the German poet-philosopher. All in all, his exposition appears to be very balanced; the bright and the dark aspects are discussed in sufficient detail, evoking in our minds a rather living image of Nietzsche.

Hirschberger's criticism and résumé

Rather unambiguous is the criticism offered by Johannes Hirschberger in connection with Nietzsche's idea of superman. If Sri Aurobindo notes that Nietzsche's philosophy is stimulating, "but solves nothing", Hirschberger comments:

> If you have a look at all the passages in which Nietzsche speaks [about the superman], we get the same familiar impression: the task is set, the demand is made in ever new words, there are descriptions how beautiful and great all that would be, but he leaves it at that; the

---

[45] Amoralische Kraftnatur, amoral being of strength.
[46] Safranski, 274

content is missing...[47]

So in the end there is a feeling of tragedy. A great genius has appeared in the public with some brilliant and daring ideas, giving a number of important impulses in the cultural history of Europe, without however being able to arrive at a really satisfying vision, and in the end he suffered the fate of mental derangement.

For Sri Aurobindo, Nietzsche is the one who first cast the seed of the superman concept, he is...

> the mystic of Will-worship, the troubled, profound, half-luminous Hellenising Slav with his strange clarities, his violent half-ideas, his rare gleaming intuitions that came marked with the stamp of an absolute truth and sovereignty of light.[48]

In the last chapter of his study Safranski points out that Nietzsche's philosophy of life paved the way in Germany before the First World War "for the powerful influence of Bergson's philosophy, and in turn France became receptive for Nietzsche through Bergson,"[49] – a statement which serves as a good transition to the next chapter.

---

[47] *Geschichte der Philosophie*, II,516
[48] *Essays in Philosophy and Yoga*, The Superman, 151
[49] *Safranski*, 540

H. Bergson

8

Bergson and the Intuition

[Bergson] seems to have some perception of the dynamic creative intuition involved in Life, but none of the truly suprarational intuition above.[1]

Henri Bergson (1859-1941) was one of the most important philosophers in the first half of the 20th century, dominating French philosophy for several decades. At times he was so popular that some of his titles got print-runs normally only reached by novels. He became especially well-known through his word coining *élan vital* which might be best translated as vital impetus. Thus he is a prominent representative of the philosophy of life, taking the view that human reason can only understand the rigidity of inorganic nature, but not life, which is characterized by creative activity, and incomprehensible through conception, though prehensible through intuition.

One important point of his doctrine is the rejection of a psychophysical identification of consciousness and brain activity: "The physical is [with Bergson] at best a condition or precondition, but not carrier and cause of consciousness."[2] Generally, in his philosophy he opposes mechanism and materialism, which was felt to be a great act of release by like-minded thinkers. He retransforms life into creative streaming and frees it from narrowing superficial analytics that deprives humans of their freedom and spontaneity.

Also characteristic of his philosophy is a new concept of time. He rejects Newton's always evenly flowing time as an artificial physico-astronomical construction which is not the real time. Real is the human time which he calls *la durée*, duration. Through it he refers to the steady flowing which constitutes our lives. Nothing is getting lost in the process, but everything keeps growing, and whatever will come in

---

[1] Sri Aurobindo, *Letters on Yoga I*, 374
[2] Hirschberger, *Geschichte der Philosophie II*,574

the future, is co-determined and pervaded by whatever already exists. Time as experienced by humans is, in Bergson's eyes, unique at every moment, never repeatable in the same way. Intuition is the entering through sympathy into liveliness and, connected with it, true freedom.

Hirschberger describes the phenomenon of life from Bergson's viewpoint as an infinite wave spreading out from a centre. Everywhere in the circuit it comes more or less to a standstill, but at one point the barriers are broken through and the impulse is able to unfold itself freely – in humans. "Only in humans," says Bergson, "consciousness has pursued its path, they continue their life movement without limits." In plants and animals too lines of development can be discerned, with first signs of consciousness already recognizable in plants, the instinct in insects, and some rudimentary reason in vertebrae. But it is only in humans that a horizon of true freedom and infinite spontaneity opens up.

It is quite evident that with this position Bergson is on the one hand very far from the descent theory of Darwin, and on the other hand close to German idealism. In the latter Schelling had declared that in the world process life and mind (*Geist*) could only develop, because they had always been there from the beginning, "ultimately achieving their self-finding in humans in freedom and creativity," explains Hirschberger. "And in order to keep the *élan vital* as infinite impulse free from all restrictions, Bergson rejects, along with the mechanism [of the descent theory], also the teleology,[3] which in his opinion is part of reason. Life and its creativity are the soul of Being, and that is sufficient." For Bergson man "is" not, but he becomes, in the same way as God, who is "a being in the becoming, incessant life, pure activity, pure freedom."[4]

This philosophy raises questions such as the following: What is it that gives direction to life, especially a higher direction in the ethical or spiritual sense, if there is no ideal sphere of values from which goals can be derived? The dynamics released by Bergson seem to mean intensity, but not necessarily increasing quality. However, we get a somewhat different impression from the exposition of Safranski,

---

[3] The doctrine that phenomena move towards certain goals of self-realization.. (W.H.)
[4] *Hirschberger,* 576

to whom we return once more, as he refers to the French thinker in connection with his study of Nietzsche. He mentions Bergson's title *Creative Evolution* (*L'Évolution créatrice*), published in 1907 and conceived as a critical contribution to an evolutionary theory which Bergson held to be too deterministic. This title was one of his most popular books, securing his ranking among the most important philosophical authors of France.

Safranski says that Bergson developed a philosophy of the creative will, but stayed away from terms such as "Will to Power". Then he makes a valuable observation: "For Bergson, as for Nietzsche, cosmic events unfold in a circular fashion, but what Bergson had in mind was more along the lines of an upward spiral."[5] This statement is significant insofar as we had already pointed out with reference to Sri Aurobindo's evolutionary theory that he assumed not a linear, but rather a spiral development.[6] Safranski further says that Nietzsche did not properly succeed in connecting the cosmic recurrence of the same with the dynamics of progression. In contrast, Bergson was able to conceive time as a creative and dynamic force by envisioning it not as stage for the drama, but as an actor who is part of it. "Humans do not just experience time, but they bring forth time through their actions. The inner organ of time is initiative and spontaneity."[7]

Sri Aurobindo's commentaries

After this introduction into some basic thoughts of Bergson's philosophy we will now investigate Sri Aurobindo's commentaries. He mentions the Frenchman several times in his works, writing for instance in *The Renaissance in India*, "… and though the thought of Nietzsche, of Bergson and of James has recently touched more vitally just a few minds here and there, their drift is much too externally pragmatic and vitalistic to be genuinely assimilable by the Indian spirit."[8] There are also several statements in those of his letters which he wrote in response to a correspondent who quoted some passages from Bergson's

---

[5] *Safranski*, 341
[6] See chapter *Hegel*, Sri Aurobindo's philosophy of history.
[7] *Safranski*, 341
[8] *The Renaissance in India*, 27

writings, added his own commentaries and requested Sri Aurobindo for his appraisal. The following are his most relevant utterances:

I have not read [Bergson] sufficiently to pronounce. So far as I know, he seems to have some perception of the dynamic creative intuition involved in Life, but none of the truly suprarational intuition above. If so, his Intuition which he takes to be the sole secret of things is only a secondary manifestation of something transcendent which is itself only the "rays of the Sun".

Instinct and intuition as described by [Bergson] are vital, but it is possible to develop a corresponding mental intuition, and that is probably what he suggests – and which depends not on thought but a sort of mental direct contact with things. This is not exactly mysticism, though it is a first step towards it.

No, [Bergson's élan vital] is not the Supramental. But Bergson's "intuition" seems to be a Life Intuition which is of course the Supramental fragmented and modified to act as a Knowledge in "Life-in-Matter". I can't say definitively yet, but that is the impression it gave me.

[Bergson's élan vital:] Not Sachchidananda but Chit-shakti in the disguise of Pranashakti.[9] Bergson is, I believe, a vitalist (as opposed to a materialist on one side and an idealist on the other) with a strong perception of Time (in Upanishadic times they speculated whether Time was not the Brahman and some schools held that idea). So for him Brahman = Consciousness-Force = Time-Force = Life-Force. But the last two he sees vividly, while the first which is the real thing behind creation he sees very dimly.[10]

Intuition and Consciousness-Force

We can gather from Sri Aurobindo's answers that his correspondent

---

[9] That is to say, not Existence-Consciousness-Bliss, but Consciousness-Force in the disguise of vital Force. (W.H.)
[10] *Letters on Yoga I*, 374f

assumed very substantial parallels in both philosophies, whereas he himself is more reserved. The subject is primarily intuition, which is differently conceived by Bergson. While with Sri Aurobindo the process is a spontaneous reception of an inspiration from higher, overmental planes, Bergson has a complex process of "sympathy" in mind. "Bergsonian intuition then consists in entering into the thing, rather than going around it from the outside," says the Stanford Encyclopedia of Philosophy. At first there is an entering into ourselves, our own "duration", and this sympathizing with oneself enables the sympathizing with others. My own "duration" is part of *the duration itself*. From this part I can "dilate" or "enlarge" and move into other durations. "But," the Encyclopedia continues, "this starting point in a part implies – and Bergson himself never seems to realize this – that intuition never gives us absolute knowledge of *the whole of the duration, all the component parts of the duration*." Accordingly, we always only get access to a contracted part. Nevertheless, Bergson speaks of an "integral" experience, as one should make an effort, "to dilate one's duration into a continuous heterogeneity," points out the Encyclopedia.[11]

These deliberations confirm Sri Aurobindo's speaking of a "fragmented" supramental, because what is missing with Bergson is the spontaneous holism of Sri Aurobindo's hypothesis. What unites both of them, is the conviction that intellectual analytics cannot achieve absolute knowledge and is therefore bound to remain unsatisfying. Bergson's intention was especially to overcome Kant; in his eyes, "Kant's philosophy is scandalous, since it eliminates the possibility of absolute knowledge and mires metaphysics in antinomies." From the viewpoint of the French philosopher it is necessary to go beyond the divisions of the different schools of philosophy such as rationalism, idealism and realism. "Philosophy, for Bergson, does not consist in choosing between concepts and in taking sides. These antinomies of concepts and positions, according to him, result from the normal or habitual way our intelligence works."[12]

Another subject in Sri Aurobindo's correspondence is the *élan*

---

[11] Lawlor, Leonard and Moulard Leonard, Valentin, "Henri Bergson". *The Stanford Encyclopedia of Philosophy* (Winter 2013 Edition), Edward N. Zalta (ed.).
[12] Ibid.

vital. Here Sri Aurobindo sees the French thinker as a "vitalist", positioned between the materialists and the idealists. He also makes an interesting reference to the Upanishads and the idea of time as Brahman in some schools. While for Sri Aurobindo Consciousness-Force is central as "the real thing behind creation", Bergson focusses on time-force and life-force. Sri Aurobindo defines consciousness-force in *The Life Divine* as follows:

> All action, all mental, vital, physical activities in the world are the operation of a universal Energy, a Consciousness-Force which is the power of the Cosmic Spirit working out the cosmic and individual truth of things.

And in another place in the same work he writes:

> That Force is fundamentally the Chit-Tapas or Chit-Shakti of the Vedanta, consciousness-Force, inherent conscious force of conscious-being, which manifests itself as nervous energy full of submental sensation in the plant, as desire-sense and desire-will in the primary animal forms, as self-conscious sense and force in the developing animal, as mental will and knowledge topping all the rest in man.[13]

So it becomes obvious that Sri Aurobindo views things from a very high perspective, envisioning the phenomenon of life as an important stage in which the underlying universal energy takes a decisive next step in its self-unfolding. More intensively and exclusively than Sri Aurobindo, Bergson for his part focuses on life itself and thus becomes a "philosopher of life".

As Bergson, and later Gebser, Sri Aurobindo too had some close affinity to the subject of "time", discussing it in many places. But as it is only of subordinate importance in the context of the present study, we will content ourselves with rendering some relevant statements of Sri Aurobindo in the appendix to this chapter, thus enabling interested readers to go deeper into this theme.

---

[13] *The Life Divine*, 957; 196

S.K. Maitra's comparative study

Maitra has also discussed Sri Aurobindo and Bergson in his above-mentioned comparative study. In the following we will present his findings in order to better understand their philosophy. Maitra starts his treatise with compliments to both thinkers; it is to be remembered that he wrote his lines around the middle of the 20th century:

> If I am asked, Who is the most creative thinker of the present day in the East, I will unhesitatingly answer: Sri Aurobindo. If I am similarly asked, Who is the most dynamic thinker of the present day in the West, I will equally unhesitatingly answer: Bergson.[14]

Maitra first explores Bergson's concept of intuition, which is defined in his *Introduction to Metaphysics* as "a kind of intellectual sympathy by which we can enter into the heart of a thing and thereby coincide with what is unique in it and consequently inexpressible." Certainly it is different from exploration through the analytical reason, but what precisely is it? Bergson, says Mitra, seems to assume that we have a faculty called intuition, which enables us to grasp reality in its inmost essence. But the French thinker fails to get to the bottom of the issue. Furthermore, Maitra continues, the knowledge through sympathy as a means of getting to the essence of reality will always be merely a partial knowledge, not perfect and complete. But at the end of his *Introduction*, says Maitra, the French philosopher had arrived at a much better definition of the term:

> The last sentence with which he concludes this book is: "Metaphysics can therefore be defined as integral experience." If, therefore, intuition is the sole reliance of metaphysics, it follows that intuition must be integral experience. Here Bergson by one jump passes from an extremely narrow conception of intuition to one which is perfectly adequate.[15]

However, Maitra adds critically that nonetheless Bergson fails to an-

---

[14] S.K. Maitra, *The Meeting of the East and the West*, 48
[15] Ibid., 52

swer some questions: how is this transition from the particular to the whole effected, how do we arrive at this new meaning of an all-comprehending knowledge and the vision of a harmonious, homogeneous whole? In later works too, Maitra explains, the answers are missing. Bergson's concept of time does not help either, for "in pure flow there is no integration at all; there is no cohesion at all between what goes before and what comes after. Bergson very proudly points out that in his philosophy the past never dies, but we may point out that the present also never lives in his philosophy, for life implies some stability and some cohesion."[16]

The gap between the two definitions, the knowledge of the particular, and the integrative experience of the whole, is too large to be bridged by a kind of logic, and therefore, says Maitra, Bergson was right when after some vain attempts he abandoned all efforts in this direction. Instead, in his writing *The Two Sources of Morality and Religion* he discarded all logic, recommending the mystical path: "Go to a mystic if you want to know what intuition is." But here too, continues Maitra, new problems arise, because there are very different paths of mysticism, whereas Bergson declares unacceptably that all mystics had practically the same experience.

Now, while the Frenchman "has huddled together all higher forms of consciousness under the single term 'intuition', Sri Aurobindo, on the other hand, has distinguished five levels of consciousness above the mental, namely, the Higher Mind, the Illumined Mind, Intuition, Overmind and Supermind."[17] All these planes provide in an ascending scale higher qualities of intuition, with the lower stages being characterized by a good deal of admixture of mental stuff more or less disfiguring the original inspiration. Furthermore, says Maitra, there is not only the inspiration from the *overhead*-planes, but also from the heart level, the soul within us, with the quality of inspiration depending on the psychic development.

Finally, Maitra points out that for Sri Aurobindo intuition is superior to reason, as the seer has a greater power of knowledge than the thinker.[18] But reason can play a very important role insofar as it helps

---

[16] Ibid.
[17] Ibid., 56
[18] In this context, see *The Life Divine*, 980. "The perceptual power of the inner sight is greater

to express and organize knowledge in our "surface being" in such a way that it becomes accessible and realizable.[19]

Evolution

Another subject in Maitra's article is the issue of evolution and the destiny of man. Bergson's work *Creative Evolution* is for Maitra perhaps the greatest challenge to any mechanical theory of evolution. "It has torn into shreds all the arguments by which the mighty structure of that theory is supported."[20] But unfortunately, continues Maitra, the French thinker was equally anxious to destroy all kinds of teleological evolution along with it, through which his creative evolution lost all its creativity. For what is spontaneous movement, if not movement *towards anything*, and what is creative evolution, if it does not know what is to be created?

> Here we have a fundamental difference between Bergson's theory of evolution and that of Sri Aurobindo's. Spiritual evolution does not mean for Sri Aurobindo merely self-generative movement, but it means an evolution in which every step in the process is directed by the spirit. The spirit is also not a mere silent witness of evolution, as it is in the Sankhya philosophy, but it actively guides and directs every little movement of it.[21]

Maitra then presents once more the basics of Sri Aurobindo's philosophy of involution and evolution, which we can skip here as it had already been dealt with at another place. As a summary, he states:

> Evolution means making more and more manifest the unmanifest consciousness-force that dwells in every being. It is therefore an ascent from a less manifest condition of the consciousness-force to a more manifest condition.
> But evolution is not merely an ascent from a lower to a higher state of

---

than the perceptual power of thought."
[19] See *The Life Divine*, 74
[20] *Maitra*, 67
[21] Ibid., 68

being. It is also an integration of the higher with the lower states. This means that when a higher principle emerges, it descends into the lower ones and causes a transformation of them. Thus, when mind emerges, not only does a new principle appear on the scene, but the lower principles of matter and life also undergo a transformation... Evolution, therefore, does not mean the isolated raising of any principle to a higher level, but an uplift and transformation of all the principles.[22]

Now, Maitra continues, Bergson too has spoken of the continuous swelling of the current of life as it proceeds, and of the past living in the present and continuing in the future. Moreover, he has compared evolution with the continuous lengthening of an elastic body, with the continuous coiling of a rope. "But these similes only point to the fact that evolution is a continuous process without any break or gap. They do not suggest any transformation of the lower principles by the higher." Actually, this distinction of lower and higher does not exist in Bergson's philosophy, nor could it exist, as the evaluation as "low" or "high" could only be possible in relation to a particular goal of evolution, which however does not exist.[23]

Now there is still the question regarding the destiny of humans in the respective philosophies. Maitra comments: "The ultimate destiny of man, according to Bergson, is to be one with the life-current. As God in Bergson's philosophy is only another name for the life-current, we may say that the ultimate destiny of man is to be identical with God." This statement as such is somewhat abstract, and therefore Maitra adduces a significant quotation of Bergson in his writing *The Two Sources of Morality and Religion*, where he refers to the mystic's love for humanity:

> What [this love] wants to do, with God's help, is to complete the creation of the human species and make of humanity what it would have straight away become, had it been able to assume its final shape without the assistance of man himself. Or to use words which mean, as we see, the same thing in different terms: its direction is exactly that of

---

[22] *Maitra*, 69f
[23] *Maitra*, 70f

the vital impetus, it is this impetus itself, communicated in its entirety to exceptional men, who in their turn would fain impart it to all humanity, and by a living contradiction change into creative effort that created thing which is a species, and turn into movement what was, by definition, a stop."[24]

Bergson's text suggests that with the power of love a new element suddenly appears, which is even attributed some transformative effect. In this context, we feel reminded of the Indian Avatar who has the power of imprinting new patterns on a particular stage of evolution, or of the Vibhutis, that is humans with an extraordinary evolutionary effective force. However, Bergson's vision is different, for the "extraordinary" humans function as part of the life current, which is equated with love, and appear to lose themselves in it "as do the waters of the river when they fall into the ocean," says Maitra. He considers this equating the *élan* with love somewhat unusual, and says that there are no comparable passages elsewhere in Bergson's works, where we always find the equation of the *élan* with time, which again is defined as pure flow.

Maitra adds that the goal which Bergson formulates, that is love for humanity, is certainly a high ideal; and it is also noble to consider all humans as one, irrespective of their faith, colour, sex, etc. – ideals which are still far from realization. But it cannot be said of Bergson that in his philosophy humanity has a higher destiny, as proposed by Sri Aurobindo who gave us the ideal of superman: "No one has announced with greater conviction that man must exceed himself, that his destiny is not to be mere man but to be something infinitely higher."[25]

But after many such critical remarks Maitra in the end arrives nonetheless at a rather positive appraisal of the Frenchman and his philosophy:

Bergson is perhaps one of the least systematic among the philosophers of the modern age. But system-building is not the thing we value most

---

[24] Quoted in *Maitra*, 74
[25] *Maitra*, 77

in a philosopher. What we value in him much more than this is his power to kindle thought, to give a new orientation, a new outlook. The greatest obstacle to the progress of philosophy is stagnation of thought, the habit of moving in fixed grooves, a false sense of respectability which makes people shrink from trying new methods. Bergson is the most uncompromising opponent of all false respectability in philosophy. For him the only thing that is respectable is the love of truth.[26]

And this love no doubt connects him with Sri Aurobindo. In concluding, we will quote from Will Durant's magnificent appraisal of Bergson in *The Story of Philosophy*:

Of all contemporary contributions to philosophy, Bergson's is the most precious... We were near to thinking of the world as a finished and pre-determined show, in which our initiative was a self-delusion, and our efforts a devilish humour of the gods; after Bergson we come to see the world as the stage and the material of our own originative powers. Before him we were cogs and wheels in a vast and dead machine; now, if we wish it, we can help to write our own parts in the drama of creation.[27]

***

Addendum – Sri Aurobindo on Time

The following passages were taken from chapter 9 of the First Part of The Life Divine, "The Pure Existent". Sri Aurobindo at first describes how time is experienced and comprehended if looked at with a pure and free vision:

Two things alone exist, movement in Space, movement in Time, the former objective, the latter subjective. Extension is real, duration is re-

---

[26] *Maitra*, 79
[27] *The Story of Philosophy*, 549f

al, Space and Time are real. Even if we can go behind extension in Space and perceive it as a psychological phenomenon, as an attempt of the mind to make existence manageable by distributing the indivisible whole in a conceptual Space, yet we cannot go behind the movement of succession and change in Time. For that is the very stuff of our consciousness. We are and the world is a movement that continually progresses and increases by the inclusion of all the successions of the past in a present which represents itself to us as the beginning of all the successions of the future, - a beginning, a present that always eludes us because it is not, for it has perished before it is born. What is, is the eternal, indivisible succession of Time carrying on its stream a progressive movement of consciousness also indivisible. Duration then, eternally successive movement and change in Time, is the sole absolute. Becoming is the only being.[28]

This kind of perception may appear natural to us, but from Sri Aurobindo's viewpoint it is incomplete:

So long as the intuition fixes itself only upon that which we become, we see ourselves as a continual progression of movement and change in consciousness in the eternal succession of Time. We are the river, the flame of the Buddhist illustration. But there is a supreme experience and supreme intuition by which we go back behind our surface self and find that this becoming, change, succession are only a mode of our being and that there is that in us which is not involved at all in the becoming. Not only can we have the intuition of this that is stable and eternal in us, not only can we have the glimpse of it in experience behind the veil of continually fleeting becomings, but we can draw back into it and live in it entirely, so effecting an entire change in our external life, and in our attitude, and in our action upon the movement of the world. [29]

The following extract was taken from the last chapter of *The Synthesis of Yoga*, titled "Towards the Supramental Time-Vision". Here we find

---

[28] *The Life Divine*, 84
[29] *Ibid.*, 84f

thoughts reminding us of Bergson's concept of "duration".

If we could be aware of all the present, all the action of physical, vital, mental energies at work in the moment, it is conceivable that we would be able to see their past too involved in them and their latent future or at least to proceed from present to past and future knowledge. And under certain conditions this might create a sense of real and ever present time continuity, a living in the behind and the front as well as the immediate, and a step farther might carry us into an ever present sense of our existence in infinite time and in our timeless self, and its manifestation in eternal time might then become real to us and also we might feel the timeless Self behind the worlds and the reality of his eternal world manifestation. In any case the possibility of another kind of time consciousness than we have at present and of a triple time knowledge rests upon the possibility of developing another consciousness than that proper to the physical mind and sense and breaking our imprisonment in the moment and in the mind of ignorance with its limitation to sensation, memory, inference and conjecture.[30]

---

[30] *The Synthesis of Yoga*, 890

Teilhard de Chardin

9

Teilhard de Chardin and the Omega Point

I have the impression that [Sri Aurobindo's vision of evolution] is the same as myself, but for Asia.[1]

Nothing, as it seems to me, can prevent the universe from succeeding – nothing, not even our human liberties.[2]

Teilhard de Chardin

The earliest formula of Wisdom promises to be its last, – God, Light, Freedom, Immortality.[3]

Sri Aurobindo

The French scientist, anthropologist, philosopher and theologist Pierre Teilhard de Chardin (1881-1955) knew Sri Aurobindo since 1949, but the latter for his part did not know the French Jesuit. The main reason is that Teilhard's writings were censored and suppressed by the church during his life time, with some of them only being published after his death. However, Sri Aurobindo's disciple K.D. Sethna, editor of the Ashram journal *Mother India*, had a keen interest in Teilhard and wrote several articles as well as two books on him. In his title *The Spirituality of the Future*[4] he mentions the journalist and editor of art books, Jacques Masui, who appreciated Sri Aurobindo and knew Teilhard personally. Masui has recorded the latter's utterances on Sri Aurobindo, among them the one printed above in the first place. Teilhard made it after reading some chapters of *The Life Divine*. Another statement of his Masui quoted from memory as follows:

---

[1] Quoted in K.D. Sethna, *The Spirituality of the Future*, 257
[2] Quoted from *The Future of Man* in K.D. Sethna, *Teilhard de Chardin and Our Time*, 117
[3] *The Life Divine*, 4
[4] London, 1981

"At bottom Aurobindo does not have a really dogmatic thought. Perhaps it is a weakness, but perhaps it is a strength; for it is indeed necessary to reconsider things from their basis in order to go very far into the future."[5]

This quotation reveals the entirely different starting position of both thinkers: for Sri Aurobindo any kind of dogmatic thinking was always out of the question; even on the Indian tradition he leans only if it convinces him, if it is in accordance with his own vision. In contrast, for Teilhard his activity as an author has always been a ridge walk. Inspired by his own insights, he was forced to move within the limits of church dogmatic, which he was not always able to do and which resulted in the already mentioned suppression of his writings. It was only in 2009 that a Vatican spokesman declared: "Today nobody would be inclined to pronounce that Teilhard is a heterodox author whose works should not be studied."[6]

The turning-point had actually been reached as early as 1981, when Joseph Cardinal Ratzinger, at that time Archbishop of Munich, became Head of the Congregation for the Doctrine of Faith, and when at the same time a high-level academic debate on Teilhard's thought began, while simultaneously the curial measures against him were abandoned. Later on, as Pope Benedict XVI, Ratzinger discussed in a lengthy passage in his book *Spirit of the Liturgy* the evolutionary theory of the Frenchman, starting with the lines: "Against the background of the modern evolutionary world view, P. Teilhard de Chardin for instance described the cosmos as a process of ascent, as a path of unification." Furthermore, he points out: "Evoking the epistles to the Ephesians and Colossians, Teilhard looked on Christ as the energy that strives toward the Noosphere and finally incorporates everything in its 'fullness'... The transsubstantiated Host is for him the anticipation of the transformation of matter and its divinization in the christological 'fullness'."[7]

---

[5] Quoted in *The Spirituality of the Future,* 258. The original French text: "Au fond Aurobindo n'a pas de pensée véritablement dogmatique. Peut-être est-ce une faiblesse, mais peut-être est-ce une force; car il faut bien reprendre les choses dans leur fondement pour aller très loin dans l'avenir."
[6] Quoted in the German Wikipedia, "Teilhard de Chardin", retrieved on 19-8-2014.
[7] *Der Geist der Liturgie,* Freiburg 2013 (1st ed. 2009), p. 24

Furthermore, Peter-Hans Kovenbach, the Superior General of the Society of Jesus, declared:

> If we enquire why Teilhard's work is so important, the answer would not merely be grounded in his affirmation of evolution and the world nor in his efforts to unite knowledge and faith without contradiction, but it is to be sought on a deeper level: in the realization that Christ is the centre of the cosmos which is perfecting itself toward Him by way of evolution.[8]

And Cardinal Christoph Schönborn wrote in 2007 that hardly anyone else had tried to bring together the knowledge of Christ and the idea of evolution as P. Teilhard de Chardin did, and he added: "The fascination which Teilhard de Chardin exercised for an entire generation stemmed from his radical manner of looking at science and Christian faith together."[9] Through these quotations, we get some important key words which will be further explored in the following.

Teilhard's philosophy

Teilhard had studied at first sciences and philosophy; later he followed up with theology, acquiring a deep knowledge of the writings of Ignatius of Loyola, and he also read Henri Bergson's work *Creative Evolution*, which strongly influenced him. Already in his early essays on theological subjects his conviction became evident that matter and spirit are not to be viewed as contraries, but rather as two sides of the same cosmic actuality. While his scientific work found recognition, his ideas about cosmic evolution and the overcoming of the dualism of spirit and matter caused difficulties with his superiors in the church. The same was also the case with a study of his on original sin, which resulted in his losing his professorial chair.

Long travels in Asia with intensive and fruitful research activities in the field of geology and palaeontology somewhat relaxed the situation, but when he wanted to publish his first main work *The Divine*

---
[8] Quoted from the German Wikipedia, "Teilhard de Chardin", retrieved on 19-8-2014.
[9] Quoted from the English Wikipedia, "Teilhard de Chardin" / Relationship with the Catholic Church. Retrieved on 27-8-2015.

Milieu, he was refused the imprimatur by the board of church censors. Eventually, it was only published in 1957, two years after Teilhard's death. Ladislaus Boros commented in a preface that Teilhard had overcome in this book the two thousand year old discord between love for God and love for this world. Teilhard for his part clarified that in this book he was addressing "the dynamically progressive people within and without", that is to say humans who are ready to move on the fringes of the church or even diverge from it, "hoping to grow beyond it."

The main subjects of the book are the divinization of action, the sanctification and perfection of the world as a consequence of the sanctification and perfection of human endeavour; furthermore, the divinization of the process of suffering and the attributes of the divine milieu, its growth through individual and collective progress. Teilhard declared that through action only "half the distance on the mountain of transfiguration" has been covered. To aspire for God through all other things, he said, does not yet mean to attain to Him truly, the promised divinization takes place at a higher price, and "all that humans can contribute in the process is to keep themselves ready and to accept humbly."[10]

We may compare this with the first paragraph in Sri Aurobindo's well-known writing *The Mother*.

> There are two powers that alone can effect in their conjunction the great and difficult thing which is the aim of our endeavour, a fixed and unfailing aspiration that calls from below and a supreme Grace from above that answers.[11]

Teilhard's second great major work is titled *The Phenomenon of Man;* it was written in 1940 and published in 1955 shortly after his death. The most important theses in this title and some other writings such as *The Future of Man* or *My Universe* may be summarized as follows:

Evolution is characterized by growing complexity and conscious-

---

[10] See as a source the German Wikipedia, *Teilhard de Chardin*, retrieved on 16-8-2014.
[11] *The Mother with Letters on the Mother*, 3

ness. It reaches a summit in the brain of humans, with conscious self-reflection becoming possible for the first time. Even while the physical evolution seems to be completed with *homo sapiens*, it progresses further on the psychic-mental plane. The constantly growing population on earth with its limited living space results in an agglomeration causing conflicts and frictions and forcing us to make a decision for an organic process of unification or else accept perdition. The settling of the earth has created, beyond the biosphere, a spirit-sphere, a field of consciousness, which Teilhard calls the "Noosphere". With the latter getting more and more compact, humans become gradually aware that everything is connected with everything else, and they are supported in this perception by the findings of modern science.

As humans see themselves as cells in a body of humanity, there is a growing sense of the whole and an increasing aspiration to serve it. Individual attempts at perfection lead into an impasse, only the striving for a joint wholeness and fulfilment brings about progress. However, the individual will not get lost in the whole, but will be rather sublated in it with the capacity of personal differentiation. The self-giving is offered to something greater than himself, that is to say something beyond-human, which however is actually not a something, but a somebody, the cosmic Christ. For humans seeking true fulfilment, he is a source of strength and attraction. If they become more and more one with the mystical body of Christ, they are getting perfected, with their love developing into true brotherly love and their egocentric desires losing force.

The whole cosmic development is convergent, that is to say, everything strives towards togetherness. That is true also for humans who are heading towards a goal – Omega – which is also conceived in a personal manner. Thus there is an aspiration from below as well as an attraction from above, leading humans spirally towards perfection. The loving unification of more and more humans increases evermore the force of attraction of the goal until a powerful impulse seizes all humans of goodwill, whereupon they advance as a unified being into a higher, divine dimension.

Omega is the last letter of the Greek alphabet. In the Revelation of

John (21,6) it says: "I am the Alpha and the Omega, the beginning and the end." The Omega Point is the goal, direction and impetus of evolution, by Teilhard equated with Christ in his essay *My Universe*:

> As Christ is Omega, the universe is physically, deep into its material marrow, permeated by the influence of his superhuman nature.[12]

And again, in his writing *The Phenomenon of Man*, he writes in a more abstract style:

> If the Omega Point by its very nature did not escape from the time and space which it gathers together, it would not be Omega. Autonomy, actuality, irreversibility and, finally, transcendence: these are the four attributes of Omega.[13]

However, Teilhard made it clear in his writings that the goal of the cosmogenesis should be comprehended as something personal or trans-personal. The Wikipedia notes on this point: "As the spirit has become personal in humans, the goal too has to be understood in a personal manner, as the centre of all centred units. Teilhard did not envision the perfection of man by way of a further perfecting of individuals, but in the fulfilling merging of individuals in the community."[14]

Comparative studies

This latter statement is quite significant, revealing some essential difference in the vision of Teilhard and Sri Aurobindo, which has been identically pointed out in several studies. Although Sri Aurobindo's Yoga has been conceived as a collective Yoga which achieves its highest fulfilment only in the community, the individual progressive development even beyond man is, as mentioned before, an important aspect of his spirituality.

Nevertheless, some significant convergences in the vision of both

---

[12] Quoted from the German Wikipedia, *Mein Universum*, 40.
[13] Quoted from the German Wikipedia, *Der Mensch im Kosmos*, 279.
[14] German Article *Teilhard de Chardin*, 16-8-2014.

philosophers are obvious. Thus we find a strong turning to this world, the affirmation of life, the affirmation of matter and a loving care for it, a very confident spiritual philosophy of evolution with an ultimately irresistible forward impetus, and the culmination of evolution in a fulfilling perfection. It goes without saying that for the Jesuit Teilhard Christ has to play an important role in his view of the world, though some of his texts are formulated in such a way that they may appeal to Non-Christians as well.

In his title *Teilhard de Chardin and our Time*[15] K.D. Sethna has also investigated the question how essential faith in Christ is for Teilhard's philosophy. With the help of some quotations from the latter's writings he shows that his faith in Christ gets its full meaning only in connection with his faith in the world, but would not be fulfilling in itself. Thus, Teilhard writes:

> In future, faith in Christ will never hold its own or gain ground except through the medium of faith in the world.[16]
> I have come to see more clearly the only thing I believe and the only thing I want to be my gospel and my vocation, if I may put it so. The things in which I believe: there are not many of them. They are first and fundamentally the value of the world and secondly the indispensability of some Christ to give this world a consistency, a heart and a face.[17]

Here it is striking that for Teilhard the "value of the world" has first priority, and we should also note the formulation "of some Christ", which might be interpreted in such a way that from a high philosophical viewpoint it may not necessarily be Jesus of Nazareth. But actually he does refer to him, as becomes obvious from a later letter where Teilhard writes with reference to the giving of a heart and a face: "We cannot dedicate ourselves to a faceless world." Then he adds: "And it is because we have, historically speaking, no face to give it but that of Christ that I feel myself bound until the end..."[18]

---

[15] Pondicherry 2000.
[16] Letter dated 4-5-1931, quoted in *Teilhard de Chardin and our Time*, 136
[17] Letter dated 25-2-1929, quoted in ibid., 137
[18] Letter dated 15-7-1929, quoted in ibid., 138

Sethna deepens this theme with another, significant perspective:

> We may note that his philosophy, involving a loving and lovable Omega, whose secret presence enfolds us and attracts our adoration as well as endows the cosmos with solidarity and unity and evolves it as one whole towards ever more complex and conscious states of synthesis, has room for a "heart" in the universe no less than for a "consistency" (a holding-together) without the postulate of a Christ.[19]

As evidence Sethna quotes a text of Teilhard in which he makes, summarized, the following statement: if positive changes come about in the world due to a working together of all forces and if humans consequently arrive at a condition of peace, trust and love, then all this is so, "because the world has a heart."[20]

In his conclusion, Sethna arrives at the conviction that in Teilhard's vision Christ only plays a secondary role. Furthermore, Sethna sees the historical Christ only as a stepping-stone to the cosmic Christ, who is "but the Principle of Evolution apotheosized", representing a special enhanced stage of activity reached by a Universal Presence functioning under the appearance of an ascending cosmogenesis – "a Presence that was there even before the birth of Christ."[21] This Presence, says Sethna, is essentially the truth behind Teilhard's Christian position; Jesus himself could be considered as the concentrated manifestation of this presence rather than its individual source and origin.

Through this perspective Teilhard's vision becomes more accessible even for Non-Christians; it almost changes from a Christian theology into a universal philosophy and also gets closer to Sri Aurobindo. The latter saw Christ as an Avatar, in the same way as Krishna and Buddha,[22] and he noted in an aphorism that Christ has humanized Europe from his Cross.[23] From his viewpoint, Avatars appear on earth in order to stabilize and speed up the progress in certain phases of evolution. Although he had a special relationship to Krishna, he recognizes

---

[19] *Teilhard de Chardin and our Time*, 139
[20] Ibid., 139. The quotation is taken from a writing of the Teilhard expert Rideau.
[21] Ibid., 143
[22] *The Synthesis of Yoga*, 65
[23] *Essays Divine and Human*, 427

no less the importance of other great spiritual personalities.

Therefore, basically Sri Aurobindo's philosophy should be globally accessible, but there is a restriction insofar as some of his thoughts can only be comprehended in connection with a faith in reincarnation, which was adopted by Sri Aurobindo from Hindu tradition. The 22nd chapter in the last part of *The Life Divine* discusses comprehensively the subject of "Rebirth and Other Worlds", which is naturally of no importance for Teilhard as a Christian – he actually declined to accept this whole idea.

F.J. Korom's study

A large number of books and articles have been published in the past on Sri Aurobindo and Teilhard de Chardin. In the following we select an article by Frank J. Korom from 1989, *The Evolutionary Thought of Aurobindo Ghose and Teilhard de Chardin*, for analysing his findings.[24]

Korom starts with an interesting little note: from his viewpoint it is obvious that both thinkers have studied Bergson's title *Creative Evolution* (1907) "very closely", incorporating elements of his thought in their works, which, he says, is more evident in Teilhard's writings than in Sri Aurobindo's. However, as we had already mentioned, Sri Aurobindo himself denied having any such thorough knowledge of Bergson.

But basically Korom's approach is very cautious, he points out that there could only be "reference points", but not any claim of identical theses. The two philosophies show "remarkably similar attitudes concerning mankind's ontological status in the evolutionary process of the universe."[25] He believes that a starting point of their deliberations was the realization that their respective religions, that is Christianity and Hinduism, did not do justice to the challenges posed in connection with the steady advancement of science, and therefore no longer met the needs of modern society. Therefore both thinkers thought it necessary to revitalize their respective traditions through a new interpreta-

---

[24] *Journal of South Asian Literature*, Vol. 24, No. 1, Winter-Spring 1989, pp. 124-140. Published by Asian Studies Center, Michigan State University.
[25] *Korom*, 124

tion of some texts and through the introduction of the idea of evolution in their religious theories.

While Sri Aurobindo did not explore scientific details, as his major interest was in social and spiritual evolution, Teilhard found it absolutely essential to also discuss biological evolution: "Science is central to his conception and he spares no words to make this known," writes Korom. Next he reveals some common features in both philosophies, such as the idea of an evolution heading towards a particular goal; the idea of matter developing towards greater complexity in connection with a growing consciousness, and the thought of some basic energy underlying the movements of the phenomenal world. In concluding, Korom states:

> The key to the evolution of consciousness in Teilhard's opinion is arrangement on an axis. In his view... consciousness is proportionate to the amount of complexity. Thus, each stage of physical development is accompanied by a higher level of consciousness. Both Teilhard and Aurobindo use the terms "ascent" to describe this movement. It was seen by them as an upward development over time until the human being finally emerges. In Teilhard's words, "After the grain of matter, the grain of life; and now at last we see constituted the grain of thought."[26]

Actually, we recognize an obvious parallel here to Sri Aurobindo's often mentioned scale – Matter, Life, Mind. For both thinkers humanity is a culmination of the development, a stage in which evolution becomes capable of reflecting on itself and its processes. But especially for Sri Aurobindo it is not an ultimate culmination, as he considers humans only as transitional beings. As for Teilhard, he "also notes humankind's limitations but still grants us pre-eminence because we are the privileged species that will point 'the way to the final unification of life.'"[27]

Finally, Korom also refers to Teilhard's Omega Point, equating it with Sri Aurobindo's Supermind:

---

[26] *Korom*, 127
[27] *Korom*, 128

The greater universal consciousness that Teilhard alludes to is a collective consciousness. It is the weaving of all individual minds into one super-consciousness which Teilhard refers to as the "noosphere." Then, as a collective whole, the final breakthrough could be made. The final ascent would lead to "Omega," Teilhard's ultimate goal. Aurobindo terms it "Supermind," a force which draws all individual minds towards itself until a total unity takes place. We thus see that both Teilhard and Aurobindo envision a future in which a collective convergence towards the ultimate will take place.[28]

Here we may comment that Korom's undifferentiated equating of Omega with Supermind appears problematic, his exposition does more justice to Teilhard than to Sri Aurobindo. Next the author reflects on the role of love in the philosophies of both thinkers and discovers some agreements, whereas he perceives differences in the field of teleology or purposefulness. Although it may seem at first sight that both of them agree in believing that there is a purpose behind evolution, as they use terms such as "goal" and "intention" in their discourses, Korom holds nonetheless that "only Teilhard admits to a teleological schema behind his theory"[29] and suggests that some basic cultural differences may play a role here.

He proceeds to show that with Teilhard evolution has an orientation, there is a plan which gives a clear direction to the ascent, and the emergence of humankind is a predestined step in the evolution of consciousness towards Omega. The salvation of humans and God's role in it imply a clear purpose, which means that from the standpoint of teleology Teilhard "speaks to us from within his own quasi-orthodox Christian position."[30]

On the other hand, says Korom, "Aurobindo denies any concrete teleology." As evidence he refers in a footnote to chapter II, 23 of *The Life Divine,* titled "Man and the Evolution." There indeed we find statements such as "There is no teleological purpose in creation and there cannot be, for all is there in the Infinite."[31] However, Korom has

---

[28] *Korom,* 129
[29] *Korom,* 130
[30] *Korom,* 131
[31] *The Life Divine,* 859

entirely misinterpreted these passages, falling victim to an error which can easily occur while reading *The Life Divine*: sometimes Sri Aurobindo presents with great detail and cogency positions that a critical dialogue partner may take, which however are not identical with his own standpoint. He presents these positions in order to subsequently discuss and refute them, analysing their unconvincing argumentation. He starts the crucial paragraph in this text by at first referring to his own standpoint of cosmic evolution and conceding that the idea of an individual spiritual evolution does not necessarily result from it:

> Admitting that the creation is a manifestation of the Timeless Eternal in a Time Eternity, admitting that there are the seven grades of Consciousness and that the material Inconscience has been laid down as a basis for the renascence of the Spirit, admitting that rebirth is a fact, a part of the terrestrial order, still a spiritual evolution of the individual being is not an inevitable consequence of any of these admissions or even of all of them together.

Then follows the decisive sentence:

> It is possible to take another view of the spiritual significance and the inner process of terrestrial existence.[32]

Sri Aurobindo's subsequent exposition is the "other view", which is not his own, but that of the imaginary dialogue partner. This becomes absolutely clear from many statements in this section which quite evidently do not reflect his own position. As an example we may quote the following lines at the end of the long passage: "If evolution there is, then man is the last stage, because through him there can be the rejection of terrestrial or embodied life and an escape into some heaven or Nirvana."[33] Shortly after this sentence – after a long passage of six pages, presenting possible objections against Sri Aurobindo's position – this particular section is completed with the remark:

---

[32] *The Life Divine*, 859
[33] *Korom*, 865

This is a line of reasoning that has a considerable cogency and importance, and it was necessary to state it...[34]

A little later he adds, "... We may without much difficulty get rid of the objection to the teleological element...", and proceeds refuting objections based on science or metaphysics. Finally, he declares that the universal totality may be regarded as complete, but the material world, as actually experienced by us, is "not an integral totality, it is part of the whole, a grade in a gradation", containing "undeveloped immaterial principles or powers" that are yet to unfold. Therefore,

> A manifestation of the greater powers of Existence till the whole being itself is manifest in the material world in the terms of a higher, a spiritual creation, may be considered as the teleology of the evolution.[35]

Thus, Korom's thesis of a presumably non-existent teleology in Sri Aurobindo's philosophy has been clearly disproved. But Korom presents yet another objection, arguing that Sri Aurobindo follows that [Hindu] view which sees creation and evolution as Lila, that is a mere play for its own sake (which again would contradict the purposefulness). However, Sri Aurobindo refers to precisely this point in the following important passage, answering as it were to Korom's objection:

> All exists here, no doubt, for the delight of existence, all is a game or Lila; but a game too carries within itself an object to be accomplished and without the fulfilment of that object would have no completeness or significance.[36]

As Korom overlooks these lines in the 23rd chapter in the same way as those mentioned above, he arrives at wrong considerations and conclusions, perceiving divergences in the field of teleology, as Sri Aurobindo presumably follows beliefs of the Hindu religion. But apart from that, the result of his comparative research is quite positive and

---

[34] *The Life Divine*, 865
[35] *The Life Divine*, 867
[36] Ibid.

he resumes that "we find a number of fascinating similarities in the personalistic evolutionary thought of Teilhard and Aurobindo."[37]

K.D. Sethna's study

In 1971 the religious scholar R.C. Zaehner published a book titled *Evolution in Religion: A Study in Sri Aurobindo and Pierre Teilhard de Chardin*. Though competently written in large parts, it also contained some wrong statements which Sri Aurobindo's disciple K.D. Sethna did not want to leave uncorrected. Therefore, ten years later he responded with his title *The Spirituality of the Future. A Search apropos of R.C. Zaehner's Study in Sri Aurobindo and Teilhard de Chardin*.[38] It is a very comprehensive and substantial work, treating in great detail a number of intricate questions. In this place, only a few points of Sethna's treatise will be taken up, first of all the question how Teilhard came to know about Sri Aurobindo.

Sethna mentions that theoretically Teilhard might have read Sri Aurobindo's writings as early as 1914-15, when the French edition of the English journal *Arya* appeared in Pondicherry, in which Sri Aurobindo first published those texts that later became the foundation of main works such as *The Life Divine*. The *Revue de grande synthèse* also made its way to Paris, but Teilhard did not read it. It was only in 1949 that Jacques Masui (whom we had already mentioned at the beginning of this chapter) informed a French member of the Sri Aurobindo Ashram that he had told Teilhard about Sri Aurobindo's philosophy.

The next news came in 1954 from Eleanor Montgomery, who was in charge of the Sri Aurobindo Library in New York. Teilhard stayed only a few blocks away from the library, and one day he visited it with Masui, whereupon Montgomery presented him with a copy of Sri Aurobindo's booklet *Evolution*. This was a year before Teilhard's death. Masui gave more information on his contacts with the French Jesuit while attending a symposium on Teilhard and Sri Aurobindo in Paris in 1965. Sethna reports:

---

[37] *Korom*, 133
[38] London, 1981

In the course of very interesting reminiscences and reflections, he said that between 1946 and 1954 he had had talks with Teilhard and had often spoken to him of Sri Aurobindo. At last he had succeeded in making him read the first twelve chapters of *The Life Divine*. On returning them, Teilhard had remarked: "J'ai l'impression que c'est la même chose que moi, mais pour l'Asie." ("I have the impression that it is the same thing as myself, but for Asia.")[39]

Sethna concludes that with this statement Teilhard suggests that he and Sri Aurobindo share a theory of evolution "that sees in the future a spiritual completion of man fulfilling in a luminous earth life all the terms developed by nature of being and becoming."[40] The sole difference would be that Sri Aurobindo has a Vedantic starting point, while Teilhard has a Christian position. Sethna follows up with many more deliberations on Teilhard's statement, but we believe that with the above-mentioned lines the crucial point has been made: Teilhard perceives a joint basic concept, with Sri Aurobindo formulating it for Asia, and he himself for the West, and the basic concept is developed in the respective cultural contexts.

But while Vedanta is very open in its approach and can easily integrate such developments as are found in Sri Aurobindo's philosophy, Teilhard had to work in the framework of a dogmatic theology. Furthermore, in contrast to him, Sri Aurobindo did not have to consider any superior authority when writing his texts, and Sethna believes that Teilhard would have been even closer to Sri Aurobindo in his thought if his starting position had been the same.

All the same, some differences remain which would have existed anyhow. Thus, as already mentioned, Teilhard declined to accept the doctrine of reincarnation, he actually had some general reservations vis-à-vis Eastern mysticism. A significant point is also his reducing the importance of individual evolution in favour of a future collective development. Masui believes that in this regard there is some basic divergence in the thought of the two philosophers: "Teilhard de Chardin was interested above all in the group, in mankind. Aurobindo was

---

[39] *The Spirituality of the Future*, 257
[40] Ibid.

interested principally in man."[41] Similarly, the Jesuit and Teilhard expert Emile Rideau stated on the French thinker: "Careful though he was to preserve the difference of individuals, it is fair to say that the problem of personal opinions and the eternal history of individual persons are blurred by an outlook that is primarily concerned with wholes."[42]

Supermind and the Omega Point

In a chapter on Teilhard's "Pleroma" Sethna especially discusses the question of the relationship between supermind and Omega Point. He explains the term Pleroma in his book as follows:

> As a result of the incarnation of God two thousand years ago, the slow Godward process of the evolving world got its decisive impetus to "divinization" and the certainty of its fulfillment in the final union with the Supreme beyond time and space, which Christianity calls the Pleroma, the plenitude, of Christ – the union whose natural support would be effected by the evolution of a totalized and unified humanity functioning as a collective Person.[43]

Basically, Sethna assumes that Teilhard was inspired in his thought by the same supramental consciousness which has had a global impact on the earth consciousness in modern times, ultimately giving a general impulse for evolutionary theories in connection with scientific thought. Thus, with Teilhard, we find the "scientific look forward to a collective evolution of man into a 'superconsciousness' culminating in a divine manifold unity that he terms Omega Point."[44] Sethna considers Teilhard basically a born pantheist who sees the hidden divinity in matter and should therefore quite naturally be inclined to envision divine fulfilment *in space and time*. Although his concept is not identical with that of Sri Aurobindo's supermind, it points in the same direction. However, differences do arise due to the bringing in of tra-

---

[41] Quoted in ibid., 244
[42] Quoted in ibid., 245
[43] *The Spirituality of the Future*, 50
[44] Ibid., 235

ditional Christian dogmas.

Teilhard was rightly holding the view, says Sethna, that Omega is not merely a cosmic potentiality in the future, but also a transcendent actuality here and now "that will meet its own evolutionary form, the Soul of the World, when humanity will attain its maturity. If everything evolves the Divine, the Divine must be already there forever to serve as the magnet drawing upward and downward."[45]

From Sethna's viewpoint Teilhard's approach becomes problematic if he says that the maturity of humanity will coincide with the end of history, "a cessation of time and space, a dematerialization of the cosmos into a pleroma à la Saint Paul, giving everything a fulfilment in the Beyond alone. Teilhard argues as though for a fulfilling 'ultra-human' within the cosmos, but proceeds to identify the 'ultra-human' with the 'trans-human' in a noncosmic eternity."[46]

However, there are some statements of Teilhard, continues Sethna, in which he does set the Pleroma in the cosmos itself. Thus, in one passage he declares that the members of the species *Homo sapiens* would turn into "super-men" by being made "into elements governed by some higher soul."[47] Furthermore, Sethna adduces Teilhard's following quotation: "*Another* mankind must inevitably emerge from this vision, one of which we have as yet no idea, but one which I believe I can already feel stirring through the old mankind."[48] Moreover, Teilhard has written in an essay:

> The very first time we meet it, the idea of a super-human organism seems fantastic. Nevertheless, if ...we are willing to entertain it, and then begin to examine it more deeply, it is surprising what order and clarity is introduced into our outlook on the universe by a hypothesis that at first seemed crazy.[49]

Sethna presents some more evidence that Teilhard had sometimes a future development in the form of a super-humanity as terrestrial ful-

---

[45] Ibid., 236
[46] Ibid.
[47] Quoted in ibid., 236. See also Teilhard de Chardin, *Human Energy,* New York 1971, p. 63
[48] Quoted in ibid., 237. See also Teilhard de Chardin, *Activation of Energy,* London 1970, p. 74
[49] Quoted in ibid., 238. *Activation of Energy,* 68

filment in mind, that is to say, instead of an exit from the planet a change on earth – an idea through which he comes closer to Sri Aurobindo. But Sethna points out that as a rule the extracosmic version of Teilhard's thought prevails, precisely in accordance with his given background of Christian faith.

G. Mourgue's study

The approach of the French author Gérard Mourgue is different from that of Sethna and other authors. In his title *Sri Aurobindo et Teilhard de Chardin*[50] he expresses equal appreciation of the thought of both thinkers, exploring their philosophies through a kind of meditation and seeking for common points rather than differences. His book is like a living affirmation of Teilhard's above-mentioned statement on his and Sri Aurobindo's common vision of evolution. Mourgue tries to feel as it were the vibrations of the texts, sensing their affinity on a suprarational plane. Only at the end of his book, in a section titled "Similarities and Divergences", he presents a short comparative reflection.

Both authors, he says, share the knowledge of the works of Bergson and the idea of human progress, whose stages are matter, life, mind. Their goal is something beyond the human. However, humanity in Sri Aurobindo's philosophy achieves this final phase of its evolution through the status of superman, reminding us of Nietzsche, though in Sri Aurobindo's case characterized by a higher development of consciousness.

"For Teilhard, on the other hand, the final phase is the convergence towards the Point Omega: the ecstasy in God. The perspectives of the one are terrestrial, of the other ultra-terrestrial. For Sri Aurobindo, the personality of each human being remains preserved in its wholeness, whereas with Teilhard, the persons gather in the heart of a supreme Person: the mystical body of Christ."[51]

---

[50] Paris, 1993
[51] *G. Mourgue*, 162

Jean Gebser

10

Jean Gebser and the Invisible Origin

In a tremendous leap he made up, within a few decades, for those five hundred years that we have lived through since the Renaissance.[1]

Jean Gebser on Sri Aurobindo

The cultural philosopher and author Jean Gebser was born in 1905 in Posen,[2] Germany, and died in 1973 in his adopted country, Switzerland. He lived for long periods of time in Italy, France and Spain and undertook many journeys, including to India. C.G. Jung was one of his prominent friends, and he made the acquaintance of personalities such as Picasso and A. Malraux. Gebser attained some reputation through his research in the field of consciousness, his title *The Ever-Present Origin* is considered to be a standard work on the subject of "time consciousness". It is a key idea of his cultural philosophy that the present time is an age of change leading toward a break-through into a new consciousness. This is a common idea today, but we have to consider that Gebser wrote his most important works half a century ago and that it is his special merit that he was a pioneer of the new thinking.

For comparative studies Gebser is of great importance, because he not only knew of Sri Aurobindo, but was – according to his own statement – also in a certain way under his influence. In his title *The Invisible Origin* he refers several times to Sri Aurobindo, and the same is true for his title *Asia smiles differently*.[3] However, it has to be emphasized that he wrote his above-mentioned main work before coming to know of Sri Aurobindo. It was only later, when he studied his writings, that he became aware of the affinity and assumed, as we shall

---

[1] *Asien lächelt anders*, 215
[2] Today a town in Western Poland. At the time of Gebser's birth it belonged to Germany.
[3] *Der unsichtbare Ursprung*, Olten 1970; *Asien lächelt anders*, Frankfurt 1968

see, that there was an invisible influence even in the earlier period.

As he has repeatedly referred to Sri Aurobindo, it appears natural to approach Gebser and his thought via the respective titles. However, it will not be our intention to introduce his complete philosophy, but only a small part of it which is especially relevant in the context of comparative studies

The Invisible Origin

"The book describes evolution as re-enactment, future becomes visible in the present. There arise fascinating vistas on humans in the totality of Life" – that is how the content of the book is put in a nutshell on the cover. This basic thought is then elaborated upon by the author in more detail: it is only in the reality structure of the world of concepts that evolution can be described as progression, says Gebser, but there is a deeper plane of the invisible where the occurrences are truly grounded, without however being therefore "causally bound". From the viewpoint of this plane, evolution is a re-enactment, namely of something that is already "pre-decided". From this results the thesis:

> The foundation of evolution is that it has been pre-decided in the invisible; to realize this pre-decision by way of re-enactment in the visible is our mission. From this viewpoint, evolution is neither progress nor development, but rather the crystallizing of the invisible in the visible, which has to be achieved through authentic effort.[4]

Gebser is aware of the fact that this is a very new standpoint, perhaps even disturbing for some readers, and therefore he clarifies: "This is not to say that other views become less valid." What he wants to present is a new, broadening perspective which, he says, can well be harmonized with others such as the scientific. Like Sri Aurobindo's approach, his too is synthetic, holistic. He does not reject other ideas but tries to integrate them in the framework of the Great Whole, showing their potentials as well as limits. The conventional theory of evolution only covers "half the reality", that is only the visible and ascer-

---

[4] *Der unsichtbare Ursprung,* 10

tainable. The complete reality, says Gebser, should also include that half which is invisible to us. If this is done, there results, as mentioned above, the process of the re-enactment of that which is pre-decided, which is to be understood as complementary to the concept of evolution as forward movement. "The two perspectives complete each other as the two poles of Yin and Yang... form a whole."[5]

Next Gebser undertakes a journey into Non-Time before Time, the unthinkable as it were before the big bang. Some sages of the past tried to express it in words, as for example Augustin (354-430) who declared: "Assuredly, the world was made not in time, but simultaneously with time. Prior to the world Time could not be, because there was no creature by whose movement time could pass." Furthermore, Gebser refers to the concept of Tao as "the divine or Godly world spirit or world ground containing and effecting the origin", and to an apocryphal utterance of Christ, who told his disciples: "I chose you before the earth originated"; and finally he adds several quotations from the Bible, such as "before the earth was formed", "before the time of the world" or "before the world existed".[6] Gebser approaches these quotations cautiously, using them as an invitation to go deeper in exploring the spiritual origin of humans, as the evoking of a memory they have lost over time. He also points out that these quotations have hardly ever been discussed in theological literature.

Gebser assumes that one reason could be the fear that they may possibly question the concept of human freedom of will. In modern language we may formulate the problem as follows: if the computer program was written even before Time and if now its codes in the form of image and language move over the three-dimensional screen – in that case, how could there be any scope left for individual freedom? In this kind of hypothesis humans might indeed lose their self-determination and freedom. However, the same problem would arise with any kind of concept involving involution and evolution, therefore also with Sri Aurobindo.

Accordingly, in integral literature this whole question of freedom and determination has been discussed by some authors. The solution

---

[5] Ibid., 12
[6] See ibid., 22

here is not found in an "either – or", but rather in an "as well as". Many of our patterns of behaviour and decisions are predetermined by outer circumstances and our inner conditioning due to education and other influences. A first step towards freedom is the becoming aware of these factors, developing the "witness-self", as Sri Aurobindo calls it. Thus we develop detachment from impulses that are generated with a kind of mechanical force, and gradually gain access to the plane of freedom, which might be worked out through soul and spirit on the heart level or on the higher planes beyond mind. From Sri Aurobindo's perspective, freedom in the highest sense means acting out of the supramental consciousness, in tune with the divine Will, in the Light-Space of Love, Knowledge, Harmony and inexhaustible Creativity. But freedom also includes the possibility of making a decision to choose Evil, which often takes place in the lower stages of evolution.

This term "decision" is of great importance for Gebser. For him the notion of "freedom of will" makes sense only if it is understood to be freedom of decision. The real decisions, he believes, have already been made in "pre-earthly time". "What is left to us, is living according to this pre-decision; to do so or not to do so is our freedom or lack of freedom." And he adds: "We do not actually live without freedom of decision, for our whole life especially consists in being faithful to that decision which had once been made in the invisible and in all freedom."[7]

The essence of Gebser's idea seems to be that on the invisible plane for every life something like an ideal line has been predefined, the authentic course of life, as it were. But due to egoistic thought and action we deviate from this line. He refers to the phrase, "he remained true to himself", which, he says, is meant in a positive sense, referring to non-egoistic behaviour – a statement which is problematic from our viewpoint because "staying true to oneself" can also mean, under certain circumstances, getting stuck in backwardness. Sri Aurobindo would write instead, "to be faithful to the Divine" or "to be faithful to the soul", that is living and acting in accordance with the inner Truth.

But perhaps that might be what Gebser too has in mind, for he

---

[7] Ibid., 34-35

mentions, among others, the example of Saulus becoming Paulus, by changing for the better in accordance with the pre-decision, being faithful to it as it were, and thus achieving true development instead of holding fast to the old self. In this sense the "participation in the invisible origin that forever constitutes all of us" is a main concern for Gebser. It seems to be marked by optimism in so far as he assumes offhand that reflection on the origin takes us automatically to the *true* source.

Generally speaking, we have the impression that the element of determinism is more distinct with Gebser than with Sri Aurobindo. However, in the latter's work too we find passages such as the following in his epic *Savitri*, in which at least a certain spatio-temporal framework is described as already preset. The subject of the scene is princess Savitri who is searching for a bridegroom and who will soon meet her future husband Satyavan:

> But now the *destined* spot and hour were close;
> Unknowing she had neared her nameless goal.
> For though a dress of blind and devious chance
> Is laid upon the work of all-wise Fate,
> Our acts interpret an omniscient Force
> That dwells in the compelling stuff of things,
> *And nothing happens in the cosmic play*
> *But at its time and in its foreseen place.*[8]

"Fore-seen" writes Sri Aurobindo, that is to say "previously seen", which again implies that it must have pre-existed as it were as an image that can be viewed from a higher plane.[9] This whole scene is significant in the context of Gebser's statements as it illustrates what he has in mind: it takes us into a *present*, that is Savitri in search of a suitable partner matching her stature; simultaneously there is a future in the air as an invisible presence to which everything heads and

---

[8] *Savitri*, 389
[9] In this context, also compare Sri Aurobindo's following two aphorisms: „Fate is God's foreknowledge outside Space and Time of all that in Space and Time shall yet happen; what He has foreseen, Power and Necessity work out by the conflict of forces." "Because God has willed and foreseen everything, thou shouldst not therefore sit inactive and wait upon His providence, for thy action is one of His chief effective forces..." (*Essays Divine and Human*, 438)

which in truth determines what happens. For this reason Gebser calls evolution re-enactment, although it is of course, from the perspective of actual human experience, development as well.

However, the basic theme in Sri Aurobindo's spiritual epic is freedom and transformation, challenging Death and overcoming the apparently ineluctable terrestrial law of suffering and tragedy. When Narad, messenger of the Gods, proclaims that it will be the fate of Savitri's bridegroom Satyavan to die after exactly one year, she reacts unperturbed: "I am stronger than death and greater than my fate."[10] Certainly, this too could be interpreted, from Gebser's viewpoint, as re-enactment of something predefined on a higher plane. Moreover, it would be wrong to believe that he pleads for a timid resignation to fate. There is a significant passage in his title *Asia Smiles Differently*, in which he clarifies his position:

> While Western man trusts his own force, given by God or the Divine, and dares to take his fate into his own hands out of this ego-strong inner security and certainty, the Asian remains dependent on overpowering fate. According to the standpoint you take, you may call the Asian attitude bondage, fatalism, or else a miracle-believing bond and embeddedness in an undifferentiated otherworldly-this-worldly occurrence. However, today this latter faith has in most cases only little to do with the former power of the magical-mythical consciousness. That power is only still active in those few sages and saints of the East, or has been reawakened by them, who succeeded in re-walking the path back into the mystical merging into the cosmos, the ground of the world – a path which, if we Western people try to follow it, amounts to a betrayal of those forces of consciousness that we have acquired in millennial training thanks to Christianity, which means that every effort to revert this wakefulness of the mental consciousness would amount to a sin.[11]

We have to note of course that Gebser's remarks on "the Asian" are of a very general nature and do not specifically apply to Sri Aurobindo

---

[10] *Savitri*, 432
[11] *Asien lächelt anders*, 82

and others. We have especially quoted the passage here because of his phrase "dares to take fate into his own hands", which should help to avoid misunderstanding his philosophy as a mere passive acceptance of predetermined data.

We will return now to Gebser's title *The Invisible Origin*. In the next chapters he discusses the subjects "Core Dreams" and "Nuclear Processes". He points out that dreams may have significant content even if afterwards we are unable to reconstruct them in a fixed order of scenes following one after the other. According to his interpretation, this experience reflects the "simultaneousness-structure of the invisible origin", which is a characteristic of the origin insofar as the latter is timeless prior to all time, but latently containing in itself the three phases of terrestrial time. He discovers a similar parallel in nuclear physics, referring to some statements of Heisenberg on time-space-"blurring" in the field of elementary particles.

Next follows an exposition on premonitions which humans sometimes experience and dismiss as mere accident if they come true, whereas they are actually "foreordinations"[12] from Gebser's viewpoint. However, such correlations can only become effective if the individual is trustfully, and free from fixed intention, "within the order", as Gebser calls it:

> Then the events occurring to him correspond to his pre-decision which, implanted in him from the Invisible as it were, is the basic chord of his life, arisen from the Divine – no matter whether that chord may be of a tragic or blissful nature.[13]

After some more deliberations, we find Sri Aurobindo mentioned for a first time. Gebser includes him in an enumeration of well-known personalities who support his thesis through various statements, among them C.G. Jung, A. Huxley, Cézanne, Rilke and Musil. He introduces Sri Aurobindo as a philosopher, "who is much more than a philosopher."[14]

We will skip now this very remarkable compilation of significant

---

[12] Fügungen, acts of providence.
[13] *Der unsichtbare Ursprung*, 34
[14] Ibid., 57

utterances of these persons on the subject of future-presence and mention only briefly, as an example, Rilke's lines: "Wishes are memories coming from our future."[15] Lou Albert-Lasard interpreted them in the sense that the future is already contained in the present as it were, "even if veiled, yet effective. What we call future, is in the same way effective as that which we call past. Both of them united in us, form the full, eternal present."[16]

In a long passage Gebser next refers to Sri Aurobindo who, he says, has anticipated Rilke's statement in a certain formulation. But in contrast to Rilke, who probably received his lines through intuition without being fully aware of their significance, Sri Aurobindo has certainly formulated his text "in full awareness and as a result of his genuine perception of the universal consciousness." This seems to be a very appropriate differentiation, because it does make a difference whether a poet receives words as a channel as it were and notes them down, or whether a consciousness researcher expresses the vision of his inner exploration in words of whose significance he is fully aware.

But before discussing Sri Aurobindo's passage in detail, Gebser makes an interesting remark, pointing out that the physicists, psychologists, artists and other authors quoted by him above made, independent of each other, those statements that support his thesis of the development of a new consciousness which he denotes as aperspectival, arational and integral:

> It is aperspectival, that is freed from the unperspectival and the perspectival ways of seeing and thinking; it is arational, that is freed from the pre-rational, the irrational and rational forms of realization; it is integral, because the earlier structures of consciousness up to the archaic have become transparent to us.[17]

The "structures of consciousness" are in Gebser's system the Magical, Mythical and Mental-Rational. Only if their darkness, twilight and daytime light respectively form no more obstacle to the process of our retro- and introspection, "our perception of the Origin becomes possi-

---

[15] "Die Wünsche sind die Erinnerungen, die aus unserer Zukunft kommen."
[16] Quoted in ibid., 90
[17] Ibid., 92

ble." An intensified consciousness is able to create transparency and to perceive the original, "universal" consciousness, the origin. And if this happens, "our consciousness is changed into the integral consciousness due to its participation in the original consciousness."[18]

In this place we may note the use of the word "change", which indicates a transformative process – humans become aware of a deeper dimension through an enlightening act of knowledge, bringing about a change of consciousness. But how did the latter become possible? It became possible, says Gebser, because humans have exhausted their existent structures of consciousness, are aware of this fact and therefore search for new horizons, resulting in a basic readiness, an inner opening. But this alone would not have been sufficient; there was also the need of a response on the part of the universal consciousness. Thus, thanks to the readiness of humans it was possible that "the 'simultaneous'[19] arisen from the Origin, the more intensive, the universal consciousness could become effective in humans."

Sri Aurobindo, Gebser continues, has presented the same thought through his concept of an involution supplementing the evolution:

> With this formulation he outlined the event that our present consciousness is able to ascend beyond the mere mental-rational through the impact of the universal consciousness of which we know today that it is seated in the Invisible...This irruption of the universal consciousness... awakens in us the supramental consciousness as Sri Aurobindo calls it. It was already thirty years ago[20] and before knowing the work of Sri Aurobindo, which he began more than fifty years ago, that I called this consciousness which is becoming active today... the aperspectival, arational and integral respectively.[21]

From Gebser's viewpoint, the "key sentences" of well-known authors quoted by him in the previous section might be interpreted in such a way that their statements could be considered as "the response of our forming integral consciousness to the 'universal' or 'supramental'

---

[18] Ibid.
[19] Das Zugleich, that which is at the same time.
[20] That is, around 1940. (W.H.)
[21] *Der unsichtbare Ursprung*, 95

consciousness as Sri Aurobindo calls it" (and which Gebser has termed the archaic-original).[22] Next Gebser proceeds to explain his position vis-à-vis Sri Aurobindo and his indebtedness to him:

> Be it noted that my concept of the formation of a new consciousness, of which I became aware by a flash-like intuition in the winter of 1932/33, and which I began to put forward since 1939, largely resembles the world-scheme of Sri Aurobindo, who was then unknown to me. My own, however, differs from Sri Aurobindo's in that it appeals to the Western world only and does not have the profundity and the pregnant origin of his ingeniously presented conception. I see an explanation for this phenomenon in the fact that I was in some way brought into the extremely powerful spiritual field of force radiating through Sri Aurobindo.[23]

A similar process, Gebser continues, should underlie the parallelism of Rilke's statement (quoted above) and a statement of Sri Aurobindo's on which Gebser now focusses in his subsequent deliberations – it is Sri Aurobindo's observation that there is "a memory of the future". From our viewpoint, Rilke's sentence "Wishes are memories coming from our future" should at first be clarified in the sense that *wishes* does not refer to *desires* here, but rather to *aspirations*. Then it is a yearning for something "that is in the air", as in the above-mentioned episode Savitri's yearning for a perfect bridegroom somewhere out there is backed by the hidden knowledge of his existence in their future life which is why she takes upon herself the long, difficult search.

Then Gebser quotes in full length the following text from *The Synthesis of Yoga*:

> All intuitive knowledge comes more or less directly from the light of the self-aware spirit entering into the mind, the spirit concealed behind mind and conscious of all in itself and in all its selves, omniscient and capable of illumining the ignorant or the self-forgetful mind whether

---
[22] Ibid., 96
[23] Ibid., 97. English translation quoted from D. Banerji, *Integrality and Embodiment in Jean Gebser and Sri Aurobindo*. Retrieved from the Internet on 1-9-2014.

by rare or constant flashes or by a steady instreaming light, out of its omniscience. This all includes all that was, is or will be in time and this omniscience is not limited, impeded or baffled by our mental division of the three times and the idea and experience of a dead and no longer existent and therefore unknowable future which is so imperative for the mind in the ignorance. Accordingly the growth of the intuitive mind can bring with it the capacity of a time-knowledge which comes to it not from outside indices, but from within the universal soul of things, its eternal memory of the past, its unlimited holding of things present and its prevision or, as it has been paradoxically but suggestively called, its memory of the future. But this capacity works at first sporadically and uncertainly and not in an organised manner. As the force of intuitive knowledge grows, it becomes more possible to command the use of the capacity and to regularise to a certain degree its functioning and various movements. An acquired power can be established of commanding the materials and the main or the detailed knowledge of things in the triple time.[24]

With this long quotation Gebser reaches the culmination point of his "chain of evidence", as we may call it. His objective was to demonstrate our participation in all that was, is or shall be in Time, due to a luminous inspiration, and furthermore providing evidence that we are able to have the three modes of time at our disposal due to a consciousness raised to the plane of intuition, and, last of all, presenting the thesis of "the origin invisible to all of us", which becomes perceptible along with the inflowing Light.

Sri Aurobindo's phrase *memory of the future* is a resounding, mantric expression which occurs once more in the *Synthesis* in a footnote. The latter takes us to a passage in which Sri Aurobindo points out that the term "memory" in Greek thought had a wider significance than today, implying a knowledge "which includes the future no less than the past."[25] Here he certainly alludes to the term *anamnesis* which we came across in the chapter on Plato. We had stated that this term stands for the primal knowledge in the form of

---

[24] *The Syntheisis of Yoga*, 897f
[25] Ibid., 312

pure ideas, which the souls had viewed at a transcendental place before entering their human bodies.

Asia Smiles Differently

In this second title of Gebser with various references to Sri Aurobindo the aim is to help understanding of the Eastern nature and Asiatic mind, for "West and East complement each other; they form the psycho-spiritual whole of our earth."[26] It is a travel account with many captivating passages. We will specially focus in this place on Gebser's report on his visit to the Sri Aurobindo Ashram as well as some general remarks on Sri Aurobindo.

He describes Mirra Alfassa, the Mother, as an "exceptionally gifted person". In two meetings with her he was able to experience her authentic "perceptiveness and clear vision" and felt her radiating a great force.[27] Gebser makes many valuable statements in this report, stressing that the teaching of Sri Aurobindo and the Mother is grounded in Indian tradition, but has also integrated Western thought "and contains, based on this synthesis, starting-points for valid solutions of the problems of humanity." He mentions the high level of discipline in the Ashram, the value given to work, as well as several other aspects of life in the Ashram. Finally, he pays tribute to the latter with the following words:

> In Pondicherry there is, as far as India is concerned, according to my knowledge and experience the only place where the mutual flooding through rational machine technology on the one hand, and through psycho-spiritual yoga-technique on the other hand, starts bearing fruit in the form of a luminous... enrichment for Asia and Europe.[28]

Gebser also refers, among others, to Teilhard de Chardin, stating that some lines of thought of the French philosopher are similar to that of Sri Aurobindo. "I myself have presented for decades a similar basic conception in my writings, without having known theirs at that

---

[26] *Asien lächelt anders*, Frankfurt 1968, extract from the cover text.
[27] Ibid., 112
[28] Ibid. 113

time."[29] At the end of the book, there is a section on India with another tribute to Sri Aurobindo. Gebser mentions the Indian renaissance and its pioneers such as Ramakrishna and Vivekananda, and he notes that Sri Aurobindo made a contribution to the new era which might be comparable in its cultural effects to the work of eminent European personalities:

> In a tremendous leap he made up, within a few decades, for those five hundred years which we have lived through since the Renaissance, which formed us, which gave us the detour, necessary in Europe, via the temporary exclusive validity of the rational. Thus, he the Asian, stood at the same point as anyone of our very best: at the beginning of that path which can lead us to the *integral consciousness*.[30]

In resuming we may state that Gebser was a vigilant contemporary witness, recognizing and defining at an early stage developments which were to mould in many respects the second half of the 20th century and the following period.[31] In Sri Aurobindo he discovered a likeminded explorer of the world of consciousness, who influenced him in a certain way, without however depriving him of his independence. In the course of his life, Gebser had many prominent friends and acquaintances, and also kept contact with alternative groups, but he always avoided joining any of them in a committed relationship. He was a pioneer of new approaches, opening doors at the beginning of a new era, without however exploring and analysing inner worlds in such detail as is done today, for instance, by Ken Wilber, who has received some valuable impulses from him.[32]

There is a tribute to Gebser's work in the form of a lecture by Debashish Banerji, titled *Integrality and Embodiment in Jean Gebser and Sri Aurobindo*.[33] We do not summarize the content here, as it is more

---

[29] Ibid.
[30] Ibid., 215
[31] In this context, see especially his work *Abendländische Wandlung*, "Occidental Transformation".
[32] See also the article of Dennis Wittrock: *Jean Gebser und Ken Wilber im Vergleich*. Universität Oldenburg, 22-7-2007. Retrieved from the Internet on 1-9-2014.
[33] Lecture given at the Jean Gebser Society Conference in Los Angeles, April 2013. Retrieved from the Internet on 1-9-2014.

in the nature of a piece of art that must be taken as a whole and would lose conclusiveness if presented in bits. It is deeply grounded in the knowledge of universal cultural history and embedded in views and approaches of contemporary philosophers such as Heidegger, Foucault or Deleuze. In the following we present a brief extract from the text:

…If Modernism has not been the Moses' Rod to part the Red Sea and lead us into the Promised Land, some today see our present phase of globalization as validation of the Gebserian integral structure or the Aurobindian spiritual age. Another thinker, along with Aurobindo, whom Gebser acknowledges as sharing a family resemblance, Pierre Teilhard de Chardin, is more often addressed in this regard, a non-localized global consciousness available in material sense through contemporary telecommunication…constituting the noosphere, a kind of cosmic consciousness which is presently supposed to be available to all of humanity. This relation has been forged in no small measure by the powerful poet and philosopher of media technology, Marshall McLuhan. McLuhan's adaptation of Teilhard's noosphere in the technological key has substantially contributed to the vision of cyberspace as a kind of cosmic consciousness / integral consciousness. Indeed, the argument can be made and has been made, that the principal properties of Divinity – omnipresence, omniscience and omnipotence – are within the reach of everyman today. One can contact any point in the globe with one's cell phone; one can increasingly access any information pertaining to any subject from any period of the earth's history through the press of a button; and one can control events and objects remotely in more and more powerful ways.

Yet there are two problems with this godhood: (1) it is sustained and driven by capital for the production of capital – and as such its principal object is in creating a control society of conditioned subjects whose choices in work, relations and pleasures are commodified and subordinated to the world market; and (2) it is "out there" but not "in here."

A.N. Whitehead

11

Whitehead and the Process Philosophy

> Whitehead is perhaps the most systematic thinker in the West today, as Sri Aurobindo in the East.[1]
>
> S.K. Maitra
>
> Whitehead and Sri Aurobindo were the greatest constructive metaphysicians of the 20th century.[2]
>
> Eric Weiss

Sri Aurobindo would probably have been rather astonished on learning that he has been compared with an author who composed, jointly with Bertrand Russell, the *Principia Mathematica*, a standard work on mathematics. He has not mentioned the British philosopher anywhere in his writings, but did refer to Russell several times, making some interesting observations. Thus in a talk in 1938 he pointed out that intellectuals like Russell found it difficult to tolerate "emptiness or cessation of thought and breaking away from outside interests". If they are asked to stop their thought, they refuse to accept it and at once come back. "And yet it is through emptiness one has to pass beyond," explains Sri Aurobindo.[3]

In the *Letters on Yoga* too we come across Russell a few times. Once Sri Aurobindo wrote a disciple that it is easy to say that the Divine does not exist, but this kind of statement leads nowhere – "neither Russell nor any materialist can tell you where you are going or even where you ought to go. The Divine does not manifest himself so as to be recognised in the external world-circumstances – ad-

---

[1] *The Meeting of the East and the West*, 288
[2] Dr. Eric Weiss – *Comparison of Whitehead and Sri Aurobindo*. Article retrieved from the Internet on 1-9-2014.
[3] Purani, *Evening Talks with Sri Aurobindo*, 598 (29-12-1938)

mittedly so."[4]

However, Alfred North Whitehead (1861-1947) was a different type of man from his colleague, being not only a mathematician, but also a metaphysician. The Indian S.K. Maitra and the American Eric Weiss agree that he is of great importance for comparative studies in the field of Sri Aurobindo, although there are also some clear differences. But one point that fundamentally connects the two thinkers is their appreciation of Plato. We already know those utterances of Sri Aurobindo in which he emphasizes the importance of the ancient Greek philosopher, and Whitehead even asserted, "The safest general characterization of the European philosophical tradition is that it consists of a series of footnotes to Plato."[5]

Leibniz and the monadology

Another strong influence on Whitehead's thought was the German universal genius Gottfried Wilhelm Leibniz (1646-1716), who was a mathematician, scientist, philosopher and much else. Leibniz became known especially through his monadology, which Whitehead adopted with some modifications. Derived from Greek *monas*, unit, the term *monad* had already been used by Giordano Bruno with the significance "physical and psychical element of reality". Goethe has used the same word in the sense of a living, ensouled individuality. It is probably with reference to this meaning that Sri Aurobindo mentions the term monad in *The Synthesis of Yoga*. There he writes, in a chapter titled "The Release from Ego", that it is necessary to overcome the ego-sense and get back to the Purusha[6] on whom it is supporting itself and of whom it is a mere shadow:

> The shadow has to disappear and by its disappearance reveal the spirit's unclouded substance. That substance is the self of the man called in European thought the Monad, in Indian philosophy, Jiva or Jivat-

---

[4] *Letters on Yoga I*, 355
[5] *Process and Reality*, Free Press 1979, p. 39
[6] In Sankhya philosophy, the primal soul, the unchanging metaphysical world-spirit which infuses life and consciousness into Prakriti, Nature. In the classical Vedanta philosophy, Purusha is identical with Atman.

man, the living entity, the self of the living creature.[7]

In German Indological texts we sometimes find the term "Geistmonade" for the Purusha, which confirms the connection of the term with Indian philosophy. In this context it is interesting to note that in the original Sankhya-philosophy there was only one Purusha, whereas the classical Sankhya posits an infinite number, which are associated with the respective individuals.

With Leibniz, God is the primal monad, all other monads are its emanations. He calls monads "the simple, physical, mental, more or less conscious substances; their active forces consist in ideas."[8] The soul is a monad, whereas the body is an aggregate of many monads. While minerals and plants are sleeping monads, as it were, with unconscious ideas, human souls have clearer ideas and God fully conscious ones. The individual monads Leibniz considers as "windowless", that is they do not communicate with each other. And yet God has created all substances in such a way that they are at each moment in concord with each other, by following their respective law of inner development with full autonomy.

The monads can also be described as "the ultimate elements of the universe", "substantial forms of being" with the following properties: they are eternal, indecomposable, individual, subject to their own laws, non-interacting, each reflecting the entire universe in a pre-established harmony. They possess no material or spatial character.[9]

Whitehead's philosophy

Whitehead's philosophy contains a thought which we already came across several times in this present study: everything is connected to everything else, or, as he himself expresses it: "Everything is everywhere at all times." He deliberately and openly draws on Leibniz' monadology, but introduces a significant modification: with Whitehead, the monads are not windowless, they are rather windows themselves, and that is precisely why they are able to mirror the world.

---

[7] *The Synthesis of Yoga*, 360
[8] G. Schischkoff, *Philosophisches Wörterbuch*, 400
[9] Wikipedia, *Leibniz*, Monads, retrieved on 28-8-2015

Any such theory of external links or relations, based for instance on a preset harmony, as advocated by Leibniz, he rejects by declaring that everything is connected to everything else because the whole world, all that exists, consists of manifold organisms that permanently act upon each other and permeate each other, with each entity "prehending" the others.[10] The recognition of reality too is not effected in the thinking, but in the prehension of the living organism. "Thinking is an artificial abstraction, a tearing of the life context. The latter itself is the true reality. This living, organic unity, which additionally also excludes the distinction of subject and object, very much reminds of Schelling and Bergson," explains Hirschberger with reference to Whitehead's position.[11]

Several commentators also assume a closeness to Hegel, although Whitehead himself declared to have read just a single page of Hegel. However, he was friends with the Hegelians McTaggart and Haldane and conceded some influence on their part. Maitra mentions as one significant difference that Hegel had founded his philosophy on the principle of thought, whereas the British thinker followed a different path: "Whitehead's philosophy is above all a philosophy of process and growth in time, whereas for Hegel all development is logical," states Maitra, quoting from the *History of Philosophy, Eastern and Western*.

For him it is a peculiarity of Whitehead that, without being an idealist, he strongly believed in the theory of inner relations. One of the biggest ideas which he thought to have defeated was the notion that realism must be necessarily based on a theory of external relations. "The philosophy of organism in his opinion is the strongest proof that realism not only can be, but must be based upon a theory of internal relations."[12]

Whitehead is through and through an evolutionary thinker, perceiving the world as process, though not in a narrow materialistic sense, which seeks to reduce all higher processes to the level of one uniform

---

[10] Whitehead has coined the term "prehension", meaning uncognitive apprehension. Maitra explains it as "a kind of feeling by which things are grasped in their unity and not in their isolation." *Maitra*, 291
[11] *Geschichte der Philosophie II*, 628
[12] *Maitra*, 290

process at the lowest level. Maitra comments,

> As a matter of fact, he has taken the opposite course. He has shown how without deviating from the naturalistic order, evolution can have unlimited possibilities of growth, how the greatest revelations of poetry and art are but further illustrations of the essential characters of change... present in the whole of nature.[13]

In other words: the same basic principles on whose basis matter in its most elementary aspect can be described and explained, are in the same way valid also in describing and explaining the highest mental or spiritual achievements as well as whatever shall be in the future. Thus there is something like a golden thread running through the whole evolution, and one important element in it are what Whitehead calls the "eternal objects". For from Whitehead's viewpoint, the world is not only a world of processes, but also of the stability of form. Actually, events can only be recognized as such if there is an element of permanence in them, and it is this factor which Whitehead introduces through the above-mentioned term. So the eternal objects give shape to the respective events, but they can only do so by means of an "ingression", as Whitehead calls it. Maitra explains:

> These eternal objects are beyond space and time but through ingression they enter the world of space and time. Their position is somewhat similar to that of Plato's ideas which also come into the world of movement and change through participation in them of objects in that world. But there is an important difference between Plato's ideas and Whitehead's eternal objects, that unlike the former, they are not substantial realities. They are qualities or patterns of qualities which through ingression into events confer upon them stability and make it possible for them to be recognized.[14]

So Whitehead's approach is basically platonic, though with some modification. In his work titled *Process and Reality – An Essay on*

---

[13] Ibid., 292
[14] *Maitra*, 293-94

Cosmology, he writes: "The things which are temporal arise by their participation in those which are eternal."[15] The world of eternal objects is for him the region of possibility, just as the world of events is the region of actuality. Maitra explains further: "The constant interaction between actuality and possibility is the pivot round which Whitehead's whole theory of evolution moves. Actuality is constantly moving towards possibility, whereas possibility always seeks actualization. This explains the need of their meeting which takes place through the ingression of the eternal objects into the world of events."[16]

What we still need now is an agency facilitating this process. As with Plato, here too it is God, though in a particular sense: Whitehead differentiates between the primordial and the secondary God, more precisely between the primal being of God, *the primordial nature*, and the second nature of God, *the consequent nature*. In his primal being God is the unlimited potential of the universe, it is eternal and unchanging, giving entities the possibilities of realization, and drawing them towards what is not yet realized. The eternal objects as such are abstractions requiring a process of concretion in the non-temporal primordial God, before the ingression into the temporal world becomes possible. Through ingression they change from that which is potential into that which is actual-in-time. Whitehead defines God, the primordial being, as "the unconditioned concentrated realization of the absolute wealth of potentiality."[17]

But there is also the consequent nature of God, in which he obtains physical feeling, prehension, and consciousness, that is to say the conceptual feeling of the primordial nature becomes physical feeling, and unconsciousness becomes consciousness, which takes place "through the objectification of the world in God, which means the realization of the actual world in His nature, its transformation through His wisdom."[18] What follows next, is a very unusual way of seeing. Whitehead declares:

---

[15] Quoted in *Maitra*, 295
[16] Ibid., 295
[17] Quoted in *Maitra*, 296
[18] *Maitra*, 296f

God saves the world as it passes into the immediacy of his own life. It is the judgment of a tenderness which loses nothing that can be saved.[19]

Furthermore, he says that God is "the poet of the world, with tender patience leading it by his vision of truth, beauty and goodness."[20] The first quotation above might be interpreted in the sense that God saves all experiences forever, and these experiences keep changing the way God interacts with the world. "In this way, God is really changed by what happens in the world and the wider universe, lending the actions of finite creatures an eternal significance," explains Wikipedia.[21] There is a kind of polarity between God and the world, which can be expressed through a number of theses and antitheses. Thus Whitehead says, for instance:

> It is as true to say that God is permanent and the World fluent, as that the World is permanent and God is fluent.
> It is as true to say that God is one and the World many, as that the World is one and God many.
> It is as true to say that the World is immanent in God, as that God is immanent in the World.
> It is as true to say that God transcends the World, as that the World transcends God.
> It is as true to say that God creates the World, as that the World creates God.[22]

These statements show that Whitehead's conception of God is very unconventional and dynamic, it is rather remote from conventional monotheistic Christian ideas. Actually, the British philosopher criticized that conception which "gave unto God the attributes which belonged exclusively to Caesar,"[23] envisioning him as a divine king who imposes his will on the world and has unlimited power at his disposal.

---

[19] *Process and Reality*, New York 1978, p. 345
[20] Quoted in *Maitra*, 297. *Process and Reality*, 490
[21] Article *Whitehead*, retrieved on 31-8-2015.
[22] Quoted ibid.
[23] *Process and Reality*, 342

With Whitehead, God is a God in the becoming, not presetting any final order, "but only ideals in a pulsating universe, in which order and chaos, becoming and passing away constitute the real nature. And God's power is the power of persuasion, not of deterministic compulsion," explains the German Wikipedia.[24] We may say that Whitehead presents a conception of God for the age of democracy. The patriarch or autocrat, the stern, implacable, punishing God is replaced by the tender and flexible one who moderates intelligently. It is easily comprehensible that this kind of philosophy, presented by an eminent scientist in demanding language, has appealed to many spiritual-minded intellectuals, especially in the U.S.

Finally, a brief note on the subject of teleology: we do not find in Whitehead's philosophy a kind of absolute ideal toward which a development in the totality would move. "So the ideal of creation is to be sought directly in the basic elements of reality. Thus for Whitehead the utmost possible intensity of experience for every actual individual being is the real goal."[25]

The comparison – S.K. Maitra

Now which are the points in Whitehead's system to be compared with Sri Aurobindo's thought? Maitra mentions in the first place the importance of both of them as evolutionary thinkers and considers Whitehead the most eminent contemporary philosopher of evolution in the West. And furthermore, "for both evolution is not merely one principle among many others which explain the world as it is and as it will be in the future, but it is the one principle round which have clustered all the other principles and without which they cannot be understood."[26]

Moreover, Maitra mentions the absolute monism of both philosophers, their unwillingness to accept any form of dualism or "bifurcation theories" (as Whitehead calls them). They also agree in rejecting any exclusive concept of either Being or of Becoming and consider this kind of differentiation as artificial and as the cause of many un-

---

[24] Article *Whitehead*, retrieved on 31-8-2015
[25] German Wikipedia, 1-9-2014.
[26] *Maitra*, 301

fruitful approaches in human cultural history. Apart from that, both are "forward-looking", optimistic and not tied to the past or the present, and averse to any "stereotyped ways of thinking".[27]

These are common points, no doubt, but we would hesitate to denote them as really significant. We may rather describe the two philosophies as complementary to each other by approaching the subject of "evolution" from very different perspectives. Maitra discusses the latter in a special section, analysing the divergences: "Whitehead's theory of evolution is naturalistic or from the standpoint of the beginning, whereas Sri Aurobindo's is spiritualistic or from the standpoint of the end." The starting-point of the British philosopher is the principle of a kind of feeling or grasping (as described above), which is the inner driving force of the whole world of process. It is already there in the electrons and has the power of joining the separate and independent actual entities[28] into an intimate unity so that each lives in the others. In the higher reaches it is behind the aesthetic sense of poets and artists. It is the one unifying factor, which, as Maitra explains, "moves on further to the uncharted immensities of the future, spreading a network of events or actual entities so closely knit together as to form one organic whole... But [this] cannot blind us to the fact that it is reared upon a purely naturalistic principle, something even more primitive than human feeling. The process of evolution, therefore, of Whitehead is basically of the same order as the evolution conceived by the evolutionists of the nineteenth century. It is clearly a case of evolution from the standpoint of the beginning. The higher processes are here all interpreted in terms of the lower..."[29]

In contrast, Sri Aurobindo's starting-point is a hidden consciousness-force, supporting the evolutionary ascent, beginning with Matter, and taking it to its highest fulfilment, as already described several times in this study. Everything is conceived from the viewpoint of the Spirit, which is why Sri Aurobindo's philosophy is a *spiritual* system.

---

[27] Ibid.
[28] A special term with Whitehead, in whose system the actual entities or actual occasions are the only fundamental elements of reality, though not to be thought of as substances, but rather as processes of becoming, "the final real things of which the world is made up", "drops of experience, complex and interdependent." (Whitehead, as quoted in the Stanford Encylcopedia of Philosophy, 3-9-2015)
[29] *Maitra*, 302

Matter, Life, Mind are, with different levels of development, forms of expression of the Spirit, the supreme reality, and inherent in them is an impetus to develop toward their respective ideal forms. In this sense Maitra says that Sri Aurobindo sees things "from the end". Hegel too does the same, but his idea of the end is different from Sri Aurobindo's. For the latter there will be, from a certain stage, an evolution in the Light with endless summits.

In his further exposition too Maitra analyses differences, rather than showing common points, but his notes are very insightful and worth reading because it is precisely through the contrast that Sri Aurobindo's own position can be better understood. Maitra next discusses the ingression, the process of the influx of eternal objects into the world of actual entities. The eternal objects correspond to Plato's eternal ideas, and in his system too there already was the problem of the question how they might be linked with the finite world. As in his philosophy the world has been created by God in the pattern of the ideas, there exists at least an indirect link – which however is missing in Whitehead's system. The latter concedes, as Maitra points out, that the relationship between the eternal objects and the events is external and not internal, that is to say "there is no inherent necessity for the eternal objects to ingress into the world of events." Furthermore, his primordial God does not have any actuality in the temporal world and is besides unconscious and static: "Such a God cannot be credited with the power of bringing the eternal objects into connection with the world of process."[30]

For Sri Aurobindo, on the other hand, the ingression of eternal objects means the descent of Sachchidananda, existence, consciousness, bliss, in higher and higher forms in the world. "This descent is due to the inherent nature of the Absolute to manifest itself in diverse forms." In this context, Sri Aurobindo does not speak of a necessity, but of Lila, free play, as already mentioned in another chapter; the manifestation unfolds out of the joy of this Lila. "This self-projection is a self-limitation, and this is what we call Creation. But this self-projection is for the sake of coming back to Itself. This coming back to Itself or the home-return of the Absolute is what we call evolu-

---

[30] *Maitra*, 305

tion... Evolution, therefore, means the ascent of the world from lower to higher and higher stages, and ultimately to the highest stage, which is the Absolute, or Sachchidanana Itself. Every ascent from a lower to a higher stage requires a fresh descent of the Absolute into the world. This corresponds to Whitehead's ingression of the eternal objects into the world of change."[31]

Next Maitra proceeds with a critical analysis of Whitehead's conception of God. Basically, he has no objection against the double face in the form of a primary and secondary God and does not consider it a dualism in disguise, but all in all the whole construction appears artificial to him and not convincing. The many detailed arguments which he advances in this context are complicated and difficult to follow. At this point we may note that Whitehead's philosophy is generally regarded as very difficult with its many new terms and concepts, which at times appear inaccessible to laymen and even to experts. The main theme of Maitra's arguments is the interaction between the consequent God and the world, which is connected with paradoxes that Whitehead himself has formulated, and furthermore his statement "God saves the world", which seems strange to our common sense in this particular context and is, in Maitra's opinion, not comprehensible from the viewpoint of logic. It is, moreover, also subject to very different kinds of interpretation. In the following we will give a brief extract from Maitra's résumé in which the author returns to the plane of general comprehensibility:

> The value of Whitehead's philosophy lies in the thoroughness with which he has developed his philosophy of organism. Here his philosophy is far in advance of that of Leibniz, though the latter served as a model for his own... But the greatest weakness that we find in his philosophy is that it is a structure that hangs in mid-air, having neither a foundation nor any roof. The whole difficulty here is caused by his repugnance of the notion of substance which has developed into a sort of phobia. He has even gone further than Bergson in his condemnation of this notion... Yet he feels the need of introducing some permanence in a world of flux, some stability in a universe of complete fluency.

---

[31] *Maitra*, 305f

This need he has tried to meet with the help of a series of double principles, such as eternal objects and actual entities, primordial God and consequent God etc., none of which is a substance but a combination of which can in his view play the role which in the older systems of philosophy is assigned to the notion of substance. And finally he introduces an omnibus principle, called Creativity[32], as a sort of universal blanket to cover all the logical breaches that his philosophy has created.[33]

In contrast, Maitra continues, Sri Aurobindo has accomplished the task which Whitehead set himself and was able to fulfil only partially, namely, to bring change and permanence together in such a way that they coexist in perfect harmony, without the need of using artificial means for closing gaps in the system. The real challenge is to establish a philosophy "which is at once strong and flexible, which responds to the needs of a growing world without parting with any of its principles. And what is of still greater value, such a philosophy will give us an assurance that the future will not be a mere repetition of the past but that it will reveal undisclosed possibilities which we cannot even dream of. The philosophy of Whitehead gives us the hope that in this great work the West will fully co-operate with the East."[34]

Thus, after some previous criticism Maitra in the end arrives at a positive appreciation of Whitehead's philosophy. Certainly, he is glad to have found in the British thinker someone who essentially shares Sri Aurobindo's approach of a creative, non-Darwinian philosophy of evolution.

We add to his conclusion a quotation of Eric Weiss, an American university lecturer and expert on the philosophy of Sri Aurobindo, Whitehead, Gebser and others. In a very detailed study he works out some similarities as well as differences and concludes that Sri Aurobindo was "a great yogi of the Vedic tradition… intimately conversant with the data of yogic experience – both first-hand and through a deep

---

[32] A category of ist own with Whitehead, along with the dual terms of the One and the Many. "In the reception [of his philosophy] it remains controversial which relative importance the principle of creativity has regarding the description of the world." (German Wikipedia, *Whitehead*)
[33] *Maitra*, 315
[34] *Maitra*, 315

exploration of the relevant texts." However, he believes that Sri Aurobindo's ideas "are not adequate to dealing with the intimate details of science", whereas Whitehead's ideas "were formed in essential ignorance of the data of yoga. Thus a fully integral philosophy will require a synthesis of both their systems." "In a remarkable display of the deep coherency of the evolutionary process, their ideas are so formed that such a synthesis is entirely possible."[35]

S.P. Singh's study

Satya Prakash Singh has published a book on Sri Aurobindo and Whitehead in 1972.[36] He knew Maitra's article, but became aware of it only when his own work had reached an advanced stage. We will focus here on the final chapter titled "Scientific Speculation and Integral Yoga".

In a kind of summary he makes the following points: both thinkers aim at reaching the point of view, or discovering the one principle, which would be capable of serving as "the explanation of all explanations". For this purpose, they take into consideration all established knowledge and all available facts. The facts of the world in their primary character and entirety cannot be available to us except in our own experience or consciousness. When the above-mentioned point of view or principle is discovered, its validity is to be judged continually by referring it to novel facts of life, ideas etc, enunciated by experts of different disciplines of knowledge including science. "Up to this extent both the philosophers are almost in complete agreement with each other," says Singh. "But, as regards the method of analysing the human experience or consciousness, both of them diverge from each other considerably."[37]

Whitehead seeks to analyse all the experiences of humans and his theory provides for the analysis of the experiences of even extraordinary personalities such as Plato or Christ, "but he approaches them

---

[35] Dr. Eric Weiss – *Comparison of Whitehead and Sri Aurobindo*. Article retrieved from the Internet on 1-9-2014.
[36] *Sri Aurobindo and Whitehead on the Nature of God*, Aligarh 1972. Also published as Amazon Kindle edition: *Nature of God: A Comparative Study in Sri Aurobindo and Whitehead*. (2013).
[37] Ibid., 166f

only with a view to making abstractions out of their visions" and does not enter subjectively the same state of experience they claim to have had. On the other hand, Sri Aurobindo, "takes a direct dip into his own consciousness and gets revitalized for himself all those experiences. Thus he develops the technique of *integral yoga* by means of which not only all shades of knowledge are utilized in exploring the supreme principle, but also the principle is made available for direct and immediate experience by the evolving humanity as well as by each aspiring individual."[38]

Next Singh analyses some of the divergences in detail. We will only render here his key statements:

> "One of the fundamental differences is that whereas Whitehead takes God merely as a function, Aurobindo regards Him as the supreme functionary."
> "The second point of difference between the two philosophers is that whereas Whitehead admits a complete disjunction between the primordial nature of God and the primordial world, Aurobindo regards the world as sheer dynamis of Sacchidananda."
> "Whitehead's speculative method consists in collecting data from all possible sources and making use of them in reaching the supreme formulation." "In contrast to this method, Aurobindo's *yoga* consists in the individual searching for the metaphysical reality by meditating on his own inner being. The meditation reveals to the yogin not merely that Saccidananda is the essence of his inner being, but also that the world is the mere dynamis of that essence."
> "The third point of difference between the views of the two philosophers consists in Whitehead regarding creativity as independent of God, as against Aurobindo taking Consciousness-Force as mere dynamis of Saccidananda."
> "The fourth point of difference lies in the fact that while Whitehead considers the primordial nature of God and creativity as unconscious, Aurobindo takes Saccidananda and Consciousness-Force as conscious."
> "The fifth point of difference relates to Whitehead taking the ultimate

---

[38] Ibid.

end of God's participation in the process of the worlds as consisting in supreme 'satisfaction' which is characterized as the supreme 'intensity of feeling', while Aurobindo takes the same as 'Delight' and supposes it to be born of 'Self-realization'."[39]

So far our condensed summary of Singh's remarkable comparative study of Sri Aurobindo and Whitehead which is probably the most comprehensive that has ever been undertaken on this subject. At the end of the chapter "Scientific Speculation and Integral Yoga" Singh makes some valuable general observations. Thus, he points out that Whitehead "is probably second to none in respect to the knowledge of the world." He was not only an eminent scientist, but had also a vast learning in history, sociology, psychology, philosophy, education etc. However, "due to his being confined to the Western tradition alone, which in the field of philosophy has paid very scant attention to the experience of God, he could not develop this principle to any considerable extent, while development of it was absolutely necessary for attaining the integrality in his system, particularly his view of God, which he had kept in mind from the very outset." So Whitehead included a lot of experience in his spectrum, but not the yogic one. Otherwise, "his view of God might have come still closer to that of Aurobindo resulting in a still clearer suggestion to the posterity to ponder over."[40]

Rod Hemsell's lectures

Rod Hemsell is an American educator and author who has given a series of lectures on philosophy in Auroville. Many of his texts have been published on his website, and a selection has been brought out in 2015 as a book titled *The Philosophy of Evolution*.[41] The subjects include Darwin, Haeckel, Bergson, Lorenz, Aristotle, Sheldrake and others, always discussed in relation to Sri Aurobindo's thought. Hemsell's approach could be described as entering into a kind of living dialogue with the respective thinker and trying to bring even the most

---

[39] Ibid., 168ff
[40] Ibid., 182f
[41] Auroville 2014

abstract thought to a level where it becomes comprehensible, sometimes with the help of concrete examples taken from everyday life.

There are also two lectures on Whitehead, titled "Whitehead, the Philosophic Method and Evolution" and "The Platonism of Whitehead and Sri Aurobindo". In the first lecture he concludes: "My proposition is that a philosophy of evolution can emerge in which a philosophic understanding and intention discovers the way to an active participation in the creative evolution of consciousness and becomes the basis of a more meaningful and enlightened civilisation. As Whitehead suggested, and as Sri Aurobindo demonstrated, this can be a very important and meaningful process."[42]

In the second lecture dealing with Whitehead, he points out that the latter was a philosopher who had reached the peak of rational thinking and was entering the new realm of the intuitive mind, which is a difficult transition.

While presenting Sri Aurobindo's model of evolutionary development, he also mentions the important role of the Mahashakti, the universal Mother,

> who knows the truth, beauty and goodness in the eternal forms and consciously mediates their embodiments in the becoming. She saves all by her boundless grace. In both of these cosmological conceptions[43], there is a power of vision, an intuitive direct grasp of the totality and dynamism of the interaction of these three levels of being[44] and consciousness, and it is this that seems to be the source of the inspiration for an evolutionary progression beyond the lower planes of mind. And for each of these philosophers of a higher intuition, the key seems to be a certain transcendent grasp of time. Both Whitehead and Sri Aurobindo have attempted to frame this intuition in a variety of similar ways.[45]

---

[42] *The Philosophy of Evolution*, 14
[43] That is, Whitehead's and Sri Aurobindo's.
[44] Matter, Life, Mind.
[45] *The Philosophy of Evolution*, 121

12

Modern Theories of Evolution

Modern evolutionism, in its deepest drive, is the scientific reflex of the Supermind's light.[1]

K.D. Sethna

In his essay titled *Evolution* (see next chapter) Sri Aurobindo has expressed his conviction that dynamic European thought would not stand still – he expected it to go beyond Darwinism and explore new concepts in the field of evolution. This further development actually took place, in the form of a refinement and deepening of Darwin's theory as well as the formulation of entirely new ideas, some of which come close to Sri Aurobindo's own vision and are even influenced by it. In 2007 the U.S. journal *what is enlightenment* published an issue with the subject "The Mystery of Evolution". In an article titled the "The Real Evolution Debate" its actual state was analysed, with a total of 12 different theories being described, of which especially the last four are relevant for us:

1 – The Neo-Darwinists
2 – The Progressive Darwinists
3 – The Collectivists
4 – The Complexity Theorists
5 – The Directionalists
6 – The Transhumanists
7 – The Intelligent Designers
8 – The Theistic Evolutionists
9 – The Esoteric Evolutionists
10 – The Process Philosophers

---

[1] *The Spirituality of the Future*, 235

11 – The Conscious Evolutionists
12 – The Integralists

The respective theories were not only summarized, but there were separate sections in which for instance important personalities were listed whose names are currently connected with those theories. Moreover, the editors also mention important works and influences that support them. In the present chapter we will analyse how the philosophers discussed in this book are represented in the respective sections. But at first we will have a brief look at the further developments in Darwinism and other theories.

The core idea of the Neo-Darwinists is explained as follows: "Evolution and biological complexity are the products of random mutation and natural selection at the level of genes." The editors point out that this theory remains the dominant view held by both the scientific establishment and the cultural mainstream today. However, several scientists have voiced their criticism, arguing "that Neo-Darwinism's narrow focus on random mutation and natural selection doesn't nearly begin to explain the processes we observe in the natural world."[2]

The Progressive Darwinists argue that "Genetic mechanisms are far more complex than previously thought." "The work of these forward-thinking scientists is showing that natural selection acting upon random mutations of DNA is only a small part of the scientific story when it comes to explaining evolution. The incredible biodiversity of life is the product of a more complex, elegant, and subtle interplay between genes, cells, parents, offspring and the environment than perhaps anyone imagined."[3]

The Collectivists are convinced that "Evolution is driven not only by competition between genes, but also by symbiogenesis, cooperation, and altruism between organisms." Furthermore, the Complexity Theorists believe that "Evolution occurs not simply through natural selection or random 'tinkering' but through the capacity of dynamic complex systems to spontaneously produce higher forms of order."

Next we have the theory of the Directionalists whose core idea is

---

[2] *what is enlightenment*, 89
[3] Ibid. 90

described with the following statement: "The process of evolution is progressing towards broader and deeper cooperation and complexity – evidence, if not exactly proof, that it may even be shaped by some form of purpose or design."[4] Here we meet for the first time the names of two philosophers presented in this book, namely Bergson and Teilhard de Chardin, who are listed in the section "Influences".

Along with some other names such as Julian and Aldous Huxley, Teilhard also appears under "Influences" in the section of the Transhumanists, who believe that humans must take control of their continued evolution through technological means such as bio-engineering etc. It is not quite evident why Teilhard should be included here; in fact, his name is not found at all in the further detailed exposition on the concept of the transhumanists. Perhaps the reason for mentioning him might be his powerful inspiration of an evolutionary optimism which includes a scientific perspective of the whole world of matter.

The Intelligent Designers assume that "certain features of the universe and earth's biological complexity are best explained by an intelligent agent or cosmic designer", whereas the Theistic Evolutionists hold (in contrast to some conservative Christians) that the evolutionary processes of natural selection and random mutation are not contradictory with faith in a God.[5]

In the ninth place of the editors' presentation of various theories we find the Esoteric Evolutionists, whose core idea is formulated as follows: "Evolution is both a physical and a metaphysical process and it proceeds according to hidden esoteric blueprints that are working themselves out in consciousness and matter."[6] Here we find Sri Aurobindo mentioned in the first position under "Influences", along with the Mother, Jean Gebser, Rudolf Steiner, Madame Blavatsky, C.G. Jung and others.

Next follow the Process Philosophers, with Whitehead and Bergson, among others, being mentioned as influences and Whitehead's title *Process and Reality* as one of the Major Works. The central idea is expressed as follows: "God is not a static creator outside time and space but the dynamic creative dimension of the evolutionary process

---

[4] Ibid., 93
[5] Ibid., 95-96
[6] Ibid., 97

in time and space." It is further pointed out that the followers of this concept have a "top-down" perspective, which Ken Wilber, one of the growing number of "contemporary fans" of Whitehead, explains as follows: "You must start at the top and use the highest occasions[7] to illumine the lowest, not the other way round." The editors further explain that through this concept God is brought down from heaven's unchanging skies and thrust into the middle of the creative universe; the relationship between nature and the Divine is redefined, "sparking a sea-change in twentieth-century philosophy and theology." It is the great project of the process philosophers that they seek "to integrate science and spirit into a whole new understanding of God – a whole new understanding of evolution."[8]

Next we turn to the Conscious Evolutionists, where we find Sri Aurobindo, Bergson, Whitehead and Teilhard de Chardin mentioned in the section of "Influences" and *Creative Evolution* and *The Phenomenon of Man* among Major Works. The core idea is: "We live in an unfinished cosmos, and its further development depends on us and our willingness to actively participate in the evolution of consciousness." Furthermore, it says that the representatives of conscious evolution are less focussed than the Integralists (see below) on individual transformation or the Eastern idea of enlightenment, and are rather oriented by the Christian ideal of redemption and community. Their emphasis is "on humanity's evolutionary future and its march toward a greater collective awakening."[9]

Finally, we turn to the Integralists, where we find Sri Aurobindo's title *The Life Divine* mentioned as well as Gebser's *The Ever-Present Origin,* moreover we find their names under "Influences" along with Hegel, Schelling, Bergson, Teilhard de Chardin, Whitehead and others. Thus, this particular theory of evolution is the one which has the greatest affinity to the philosophies discussed in this present book. The editors have expressed its central idea as follows: "Evolution is a holistic process that includes both objective and subjective dimensions

---

[7] In Whitehead's system, the fundamental elements of reality are called "actual occasions", discrete moments of experience that are always in the process of becoming. (Note of the American editors.)
[8] *what is enlightenment,* 98
[9] Ibid., 99

of reality as it moves toward greater exterior complexity of form and greater interior depth of consciousness."[10] Ken Wilber is mentioned as one of the Major Figures currently representing this school of thought, and is quoted with the statement: "Evolution goes beyond what went before, but because it must embrace what went before, then its very nature is to transcend and include, and thus it has an inherent directionality, a secret impulse, toward increasing depth, increasing intrinsic value, increasing consciousness."[11]

In the text that follows, the editors name Sri Aurobindo, Gebser and the Harvard sociologist Pitirim Sorokin as the three pioneers who began in the early 20th century to use the term "integral" with reference to evolution and human consciousness. In our present time it was Ken Wilber, "who has almost single-handedly revived the term integral and has helped make evolution a fundamental context for the way in which we think not just about physics and biology but about all of human life and culture." At the end of this section there is a kind of résumé for this whole article:

> But there is a great need in the contemporary evolution-dialogue for higher perspectives that can sift through the competing cacophony of voices and theories, highlighting the knowledge that is enhancing our understanding of evolution and bringing context and clarity to the discussion. The integralists show enormous potential for playing that role."[12]

All in all, we may state that the editors of the U.S. journal have done very remarkable research in presenting these twelve theories of evolution, including those which are far from being mainstream, although close to the vision of Sri Aurobindo and other intuitive philosophers. In fact, this whole exposition facilitates access to Sri Aurobindo's essay *Evolution* which was written a little less than a century earlier.

---

[10] Ibid., 100
[11] Ibid.
[12] Ibid.

13

Sri Aurobindo's Essay *Evolution*

Aurobindo's genius was not merely that he captured the profundity of India's extraordinary spiritual heritage. He was the first great philosopher-sage to deeply grasp the nature and meaning of the modern idea of evolution.[1]

Ken Wilber

Sri Aurobindo's essay *Evolution* has already been mentioned in previous chapters – Teilhard de Chardin was presented this text when visiting the Sri Aurobindo Library in New York. The Essay was written during the time of the First World War and reflects Sri Aurobindo's studies of contemporary developments in the field of the theory of evolution. It contains many significant statements about those developments as well as his personal preference for a model of evolution which does not limit future possibilities, but rather leaves much scope for the unforeseen and surprising. In the following we render his text in full length, as a valuable document of his inner dialogue with the European evolutionary thought of his time.

*

What in its principles and scope is the force of evolution and how does it work out in the world?

The theory of evolution has been the key-note of the thought of the nineteenth century. It has not only affected all its science and its thought-attitude, but powerfully influenced its moral temperament, its politics and its society. Without it there could not have been that entire victory of the materialistic notion of life and the universe which has been the general

---

[1] Aurobindo Ghose, A.S. Dalal, *A Greater Psychology. An Introduction to the Thought of Sri Aurobindo.* J.P. Tarcher, 2001, p. vii

characteristic of the age that is now passing , – a victory which for a time even claimed to be definitive, – nor such important corollary effects of this great change as the failure of the religious spirit and the breaking-up of religious beliefs. In society and politics it has led to the substitution of the evolutionary for the moral idea of progress and the consequent materialisation of social ideas and social progress, the victory of the economic man over the idealist. The scientific dogma of heredity, the theory of the quite recent emergence of the civilised thinking human animal, the popular notion of the all-pervading struggle for life and the aid it has given to an exaggerated development of the competitive instinct, the idea of the social organism and the aid it has given to the contrary development of economic socialism and the increasing victory of the organised State or community over the free individual, – all these are outflowings from the same source.

The materialistic view of the world is now rapidly collapsing and with it the materialistic statement of the evolution theory must disappear. Modern European thought progresses with a vertiginous rapidity. If it is Teutonic in its fidelity of observation and its tendency to laborious systematisation, it has also another side, Celtic-Hellenic, a side of suppleness, mobility, readiness for rapid change, insatiable curiosity. It does not allow the same thought, the same system to exercise for very long a secure empire; it is in haste to question, to challenge, to reject, to remould, to discover new and opposite truths, to venture upon other experiments. At present this spirit of questioning has not attacked the evolution theory at its centre, but it is visibly preparing to give it a new form and meaning.

The general idea of evolution was the filiation of each successive form or state of things to that which preceded it, its appearance by a process of outbringing or deploying of some possibility prepared and even necessitated by previous states and previous tendencies. Not only does a form contain the seed of the form that reproduces it, but also the seed of the possible new form that varies from it. By successive progression a world-system evolves out of the nebula, a habitable planet appears in an uninhabitable system, protoplasmic life emerges by some yet unknown process out of Matter, the more developed grows out of the less developed organism. The fish and the creeping thing are the descendants of plasm, the biped and quadruped trace back to the fish and reptile, man is a quadruped of the genus Ape who has learned to walk erect on two legs and has divested himself of characteristics unsuited to his new mode of life and progression. Force in Matter is the unconscious Goddess who has worked these miracles by her inherent principle of natural adaptation and in the organism by the additional machinery of heredity; by natural selection those species which reproduce new characteristics developed by adaptation to the environment and favourable to survival, tend to propagate themselves and remain; others fall back in the race of life and disappear.

Such were once the salient ideas; but some of them and not the least important are now questioned. The idea of the struggle for life tends to be modified and even denied; it is asserted that, at least as popularly understood, it formed no real part of Darwinism. This modification is a concession to reviving moralistic and idealistic tendencies which seek for a principle of love as well as a principle of egoism in the roots of life. Equally important are the conclusion arrived at by some investigators into the phenomena of heredity that acquired characteristics are not handed down to the posterity and the theory that it is chiefly predispositions that are inherited; for by these modifications the process of evolution begins to wear a less material and mechanical aspect; its source and the seat of its motive power are shifted to that which is least material, most psychical in Matter. Finally, the first idea of a slow and gradual evolution is being challenged by a new theory of evolution through sudden and rapid outbursts, and again we pass from the sense of an obvious superficial machinery and all-sufficient material necessity to profundities whose mystery is yet to be fathomed.

In themselves, indeed, these modifications would not be radical. Their importance lies in their synchronism with a great resurgence, in new forms, of old ideas that had been submerged by the materialistic wave. Theories of vitalism, idealistic tendencies of thought, which were supposed to have been slain by the march of physical Science, now arise, dispute the field and find their account in every change of scientific generalisation which at all opens the way to their own expansion and reassertion. In what respects then is it likely that the evolution theory will be found deficient by the wider and more complex thought of the future and compelled to undergo essential changes?

In the first place, the materialistic theory of evolution starts from the Sankhya position that all world is a development out of indeterminate Matter by Nature-Force, but it excludes the Silent Cause of the Sankhyas, the Purusha or observant and reflective Soul. Hence it conceives the world as a sort of automatic machine which has somehow happened. No intelligent cause, no aim, no *raison d'être*, but simply an automatic deployment, combination, chance self-adaptation of means to end without any knowledge or intention in the adaptation. This is the first paradox of the theory and its justification must be crushing and conclusive if it is to be finally accepted by the human mind.

Again, Force in indeterminate Matter without any Conscious-Soul being all the beginning and all the material of things, Mind, Life and Consciousness can only be developments out of Matter and even only operations of Matter. They cannot be at all things in themselves, different from Matter or in the last degree independent of it. This is the second paradox and the point at which the theory has eventually failed to establish itself. More and more the march of knowledge leads towards the view that the three are different forms of Force, each with its own characteristics and proper method of action, each reacting upon the other and enriching its forms by the contact.

An idea has even begun to dawn that there is not a single creation but a triple, material, vital and mental; it may be regarded as a composite of three worlds, as it were, interpenetrating each other. We are led back to the old Vedic idea of the triple world in which we live. And we may reasonably forecast that when its operations are examined from this new standpoint, the old Vedic knowledge will be justified that it is one Law and Truth acting in all, but very differently formulated according to the medium in which the work proceeds and its dominant principle. The same gods exist on all the planes and maintain the same essential laws, but with a different aspect and mode of working and to ever wider results.

If this be the truth, then the action of evolution must be other than has been supposed. For example, the evolution of Life in Matter must have been produced and governed not by a material principle, but by a Life-Principle working in and upon the conditions of Matter and applying to it its own laws, impulses, necessities. This idea of a mighty Life, other than the material Principle, working in it and upon it has begun to dominate the advanced thought of Europe. The other idea of a still mightier Mind working in Life and upon it has not yet made sufficient way because the investigation of the laws of Mind is still in its groping infancy.

Again, the materialist theory supposes a rigid chain of material necessity; each previous condition is a coordination of so many manifest forces and conditions, each resulting condition is its manifest result. All mystery, all element of the incalculable disappears. If we can completely analyse the previous conditions and discover their general law, we can be sure of the subsequent result, as in the case of an eclipse or an earthquake. For all is manifestation which is the logical result of a previous manifestation.

Once more the conclusion is too simple and trenchant; the world is more complex. Besides the manifest causes there are those that are unmanifest or latent and not subject to our analysis or come from behind or above and cannot be calculated or forecast though by a higher revelatory Knowledge they may be foreseen. This element increases as we climb the ladder of existence; its scope is greater in Life than in Matter, freer in Mind than in Life. European thought already tends to posit behind all manifest activity an Unmanifest called according to intellectual predilection either the Inconscient or the Subconscient which contains more and in a way unseizable to us knows more and can more than the surface existence. Out of this Unmanifest the manifest constantly emerges.

Again we return towards an ancient truth already known to the Vedic sages, - the idea of an inconscient or subconscient ocean of being, the ocean of the heart of things out of which the worlds form themselves. But the Veda posits also a governing and originating Superconscient which accounts for the appearance of a hidden consciousness and knowledge pervading the operations of Evolution and which constitutes the self-acting Law and Truth behind them.

The theory of materialistic evolution led naturally to the idea of a slow and gradual progression in a straight line. It admits reversions, atavisms, loops and zigzags of reaction deflecting the straight line, but these must necessarily be subordinate, hardly visible if we calculate by ages rather than by shorter periods of time. Here too, fuller knowledge disturbs the received notions. In the history of man everything seems now to point to alternations of a serious character, ages of progression, ages of recoil, the whole constituting an evolution that is cyclic rather in one straight line. A theory of cycles of human civilisation has been advanced, we may yet arrive at the theory of cycles of human evolution, the Kalpa and Manwantaras of the Hindu theory. If its affirmation of cycles of world-existence is farther off from affirmation, it is because they must be so vast in their periods as to escape not only all our means of observations, but all our means of deduction or definite inference.

Instead of low, steady, minute gradations it is now suggested that new steps in evolution are rather effected by rapid and sudden outbursts, outbreaks, as it were, of manifestations from the unmanifest. Shall we say that Nature preparing slowly behind the veil, working a little backwards, working a little forwards, one day arrives at the combination of outward things which makes it possible for her to throw her new idea into a realised formation, suddenly, with violence, with a glorious dawning, with a grandiose stride? And that would explain the economy of her relapses and her reappearances of things long dead. She aims at a certain immediate result and to arrive at it more quickly and entirely she sacrifices many of her manifestations and throws them back into the latent, the unmanifest, the subconscient. But she has not finished with them; she will need them at another stage for a farther result. Therefore she brings them forward and they reappear in new forms and other combinations and act towards new ends. So evolution advances.

And her material means? Not the struggle for life only. The real law, it is now suggested, is rather mutual help or at least mutual accommodation. Struggle exists, mutual destruction exists, but as a subordinate movement, a red minor chord, and only becomes acute when the movement of mutual accommodation fails and elbow-room has to be made for a fresh attempt, a new combination.

The propagation of acquired characteristics by heredity was too hastily and completely asserted; it is now perhaps in danger of being too summarily denied. Not Matter alone, but Life and Mind working upon Matter help to determine evolution. Heredity is only a material shadow of soul-reproduction, of the rebirth of Life and Mind into new forms. Ordinarily, as a constant factor or basis, there is the reproduction of that which was already evolved; for new characteristics to be propagated in the species they must have been accepted, received, sanctioned in the vital and mental worlds; then only can they be automatically self-reproduced from the material seed. Otherwise they are private and personal acquisitions and are returned into the State exchequer, the treasury of the subconscient, and do not go to the family estate. When the mind-world and life-world are ready, they are poured out freely on fit recipients. This is the reason why it is predisposition that is chiefly inherited. The psychical and vital force in the material principle is first impressed; when that has been done on a sufficient scale, it is ready for a general new departure and an altered heredity appears.

Thus the whole view of Evolution begins to change. Instead of a mechanical, gradual, rigid evolution out of indeterminate Matter by Nature-Force we move towards the perception of a conscious, supple, flexible, intensely surprising and constantly dramatic evolution by a superconscient Knowledge which reveals things in Matter, Life and Mind out of the unfathomable Inconscient from which they rise.

Literature

1. English Complete Editions

Sri Aurobindo Birth Centenary Library (*SABCL*). Pondicherry: Sri Aurobindo Ashram 1972. Complete edition in 30 vols., not available any more.

Complete Works of Sri Aurobindo (*CWSA*). Pondicherry: Sri Aurobindo Ashram, from 1995. Complete edition in 36 vols. Some volumes have currently not yet been published. Info: sabda.in / Collected Works
1. Early Cultural Writings. 2. Collected Poems. 3.-4. Collected Plays and Stories. 5. Translations. 6.-7. Bande Mataram. 8. Karmayogin. 9. Writings in Bengali and Sanskrit. 10.-11. Record of Yoga. 12. Essays Divine and Human. 13. Essays in Philosophy and Yoga. 14. Vedic and Philological Studies. 15. The Secret of the Veda. 16. Hymns to the Mystic Fire. 17. Isha Upanishad. 18. Kena and Other Upanishads. 19. Essays on the Gita. 20. The Renaissance of India with a Defence of Indian Culture. 21.-22. The Life Divine. 23.-24. The Synthesis of Yoga. 25. The Human Cycle – The Ideal of Human Unity – War and Self-Determination. 26. The Future Poetry. 27. Letters on Poetry and Art 28.-31. Letters on Yoga. 32. The Mother with Letters on the Mother. 33-34. Savitri – A Legend and a Symbol. 35. Letters on Himself and the Ashram. 36. Autobiographical Notes and Other Writings of Historical Interest. 37. Reference Volume

Collected Works of the Mother (*CWM*). Pondicherry: Sri Aurobindo Ashram. Complete edition in 17 vols.
1. Prayers and Meditations. 2. Words of Long Ago. 3. Questions and Answers 1929-1931. 4. Questions and Answers 1950-51. 5. Questions and Answers 1953. 6. Questions and Answers 1954. 7. Questions and Answers 1955. 8. Questions and Answers 1956. 9. Questions and Answers 1957-58. 10. On Thoughts and Aphorisms. 11. Notes on the Way. 12. On Education. 13.-15. Words of the Mother I-III. 16. Some Answers from the Mother. 17. More Answers from the Mother.

2. Talks and Correspondence

Nirodbaran. *Correspondence with Sri Aurobindo*. Pondicherry: Sri Aurobindo Ashram 1983
Nirodbaran. *Talks with Sri Aurobindo*. Pondicherry: Sri Aurobindo Ashram 2001
Purani, A.B. *Evening Talks with Sri Aurobindo*. Pondicherry: Sri Aurobindo Ashram 2007

3. Secondary Literature on Sri Aurobindo

Banerji, Debashish. Seven Quartets of Becoming. A Transformative Yoga Psychology Based on the Diaries of Sri Aurobindo. New Delhi, 2012
Hemsell, Rod. The Philosophy of Evolution. Auroville 2014
Huchzermeyer, Wilfried. Der Übermensch – bei Friedrich Nietzsche und Sri Aurobindo. Gladenbach 1986
--,--: Sri Aurobindo – Saga of a Great Indian Sage. New Delhi 2013
Nirodbaran. *Twelve Years with Sri Aurobindo*. Pondicherry: Sri Aurobindo Ashram 1973
Maitra, S.K. *The Meeting of the East and the West in Sri Aurobindo's Philosophy*. Pondicherry: Sri Aurobindo Ashram 2000
Sanyal, Indrani & Roy, Krishna: Understanding Thoughts of Sri Aurobindo, New Delhi 2007
Sethna, K.D. The Spirituality of the Future. A Search apropos of R.C. Zaehner's Study in Sri Aurobindo and Teilhard de Chardin. London 1981
--,--: Teilhard de Chardin and Our Time. Pondicherry 2000
--,--: Sri Aurobindo and Greece. Pondicherry 1998
Singh, S..P. Sri Aurobindo and Whitehead on the Nature of God. Aligarh 1972

Index

Albert-Lasard, Lou 153
Alfassa, Mirra, the Mother 51, 54, 55, 60, 61, 79, 157, 179
Anaxagoras 44, 45
Aristotle 15, 27, 34, 175
Bergson, Henri 85, 89, 95, 110, **111-125**, 129, 135, 144, 164, 171, 175, 179, 180
Bhowmik, Sushmita 91
Blavatsky, Madame 179
Böhme, Jacob 51, 66, 68
Boros, Ladislaus 130
Bracker, Klaus J. 49
Bruno, Giordano 50, 51, 162
Caesar, Julius 81, 167
Cézanne, Paul 152
Comte, Auguste 73
Darwin, Charles 11, 108, 113, 175, 177, 178, 184
Durant, Will 78, 123
Fichte, J.G. 48, 50, 58, 60, 75, 79, 83
Gebser, Jean 74, 117, **145-159**, 172, 179, 180, 181
Glockner, Hermann 81
Goethe, Johann Wolfgang von 50, 51, 59, 78, 162
Hegel, G.W.F. 8, 15, 34, 48, 50-52, 63, 64, **71-92**, 114, 164, 170, 180
Heidegger, Martin 15, 159
Heisenberg, Werner 152
Hemsell, Rod 7, 175
Heraclitus **14-25**, 80, 95
Hirschberger, Johannes 6, 42, 45, 62, 67, 68, 70, 72, 82, 109, 112, 113, 164
Hölderlin, Friedrich 50
Huston, Tom 49
Huxley, Aldous 179
Huxley, Julian 179

Ignatius von Loyola 129
Inge, Dean 40
Jung, C.G. 146, 152, 179
Kant, Immanuel 8, 12, 34, 48, 50, 73, 75, 85, 116
Kirchhoff, Jochen 50, 51, 59-63
Korom, F.J. 135-140
Krishnaprem 40, 44
Leibniz, Gottfried Wilhelm 162, 163, 171
Maitra, S.K. 31, 32, 78, 82, 83-86, 118-123, 161, 162, 164, 165-173
Malraux, André 146
Masui, Jacques 127, 140, 141
Montgomery, Eleanor 140
Mourgue, Gérard 144
Müller, Max 52
Musil, Robert 152
Napoleon 81
Nietzsche, Friedrich 11, 15, 18, 48, **93-110**, 114, 144
Novalis 50, 51
Odin, Steve 63, 78, 85-89
Oetinger, Ch. 66, 67
Picasso 146
Plato 12, 15, **26-36**, 38, 41, 72, 85, 156, 162, 165, 166, 170, 173
Plotinus **37-46**, 50, 62, 72
Purani, A.B. 31, 40, 43, 85, 161
Pythagoras 34, 35, 38, 46
Ranade, R.D. 15
Ratzinger, Joseph Cardinal 128
Rideau, Emile 134, 142
Rilke, Rainer Maria 152, 153, 155
Russell, Bertrand 94, 161
Russell, Bertrand 94, 161
Safranski, Rüdiger 6, 100-114
Salomé, Lou 102

Schelling, F.W.J. **47-70**, 74, 79, 106, 113, 164, 180
Schlegel, Brothers 50, 51, 53, 54
Schleiermacher, F.D.E. 51
Schönborn, Cardinal Christoph 129
Schopenhauer, Arthur 73, 102, 107
Sethna, K.D. 32-34, 127, 133, 134, 140-144, 177
Shankara 53, 72, 85, 88
Singh, S.P. 173-175
Socrates 15, 27
Sorokin, Pitirim 181
Spencer, Herbert 85
Spinoza, Benedictus de 34, 50, 72, 73

Steiner, Rudolf 49, 179
Teilhard de Chardin, Pierre 38, 74, **126-144**, 157, 159, 179, 180, 182
Tieck, Ludwig 51
Weischedel, Wilhelm 48
Weiss, Eric 161, 162, 172, 173
West, M.L. 17, 18
Whitehead, A.N. 89, **160-176**, 179, 180
Wilber, Ken 49, 158, 180, 181, 182
Wilkens, Charles 53
Wirth, Jason M. 52, 53
Zaehner, R.C. 140

International Publications

Auroville Architecture
by Franz Fassbender

Auroville Form Style and Design
by Franz Fassbender

Landscapes and Gardens of Auroville
by Franz Fassbender

Inauguration of Auroville
by Franz Fassbender

Auroville in a Nutshell
by Tim Wrey

Death doesn't exist
The Mother on Death, Sri Aurobindo on Rebirth
Compiled by Franz Fassbender

Divine Love
Compiled by Franz Fassbender

Five Dream
by Sri Aurobindo

A Vision
Compiled by Franz Fassbender

Passage to More than India
by Dick Batstone

The Mother on Japan
Compiled by Franz Fassbender

Children of Change: A Spiritual Pilgrimage
by Amrit (Howard Shoji Iriyama)

Memories of Auroville - told by early Aurovilians
by Janet Feran

The Journeying Years
by Dianna Bowler

Auroville Reflected
by Bindu Mohanty

Finding the Psychic Being
by Loretta Shartsis

The Teachings of Flowers
The Life and Work of the Mother of the Sri Aurobindo Ashram
by Loretta Shartsis

The Supramental Transformation
by Loretta Shartsis

The Mother's Yoga - 1956-1973 (English & French)
Vol. 1, 1956-1967 & Vol. 2, 1968-1973
by Loretta Shartsis

Antithesis of Yoga
by Jocelyn Janaka

Bougainvilleas PROTECTION
by Narad (Richard Eggenberger), Nilisha Mehta

Crossroad The New Humanity
by Paulette Hadnagy

Die Praxis Des Integralen Yoga
by M. P. Pandit

The Way of the Sunlit Path
by William Sullivan

Wildlife great and small of India's Coromandel
by Tim Wrey

A New Education With A Soul
by Marguerite Smithwhite

Featured Titles

Divine Love

The texts presented in this book are selected from the Mother and Sri Aurobindo.
"Awakened to the meaning of my heart. That to feel love and oneness is to live. And this the magic of our golden change, is all the truth I know or seek, O sage."

Sri Aurobindo, Savitri, Book XII, Epilog

A Vision by the Mother

On 28th May 1958, the Mother recounted a vision she once had of a wonderful Being of Love and Consciousness, emanated from the Supreme Origin and projected directly into the Inconscient so that the creation would gradually awaken to the Supramental Consciousness. The Mother's account of this vision was brought out a first time in November 1906, in the Revue Cosmique, a monthly review published in Paris.

A Dream – Aims and Ideals of Auroville
the Mother on Auroville

50 years of Auroville from 28.02.1968 - 28.02.2018
Today, information about Auroville is abundant. Many people try to make meaning out of Auroville – about its conception, to what direction should we grow towards, and, what are we doing here?

But what was Mother's original Dream and what was her Vision for Auroville back then?

Matrimandir Talks by the Mother

This book presents most of Mother's Matrimandir talks, including how she conceived the idea for this special concentration and meditation building in Auroville.

Memories of Auroville - Told by early Aurovilians

Memories of Auroville is a book about the very early days of Auroville based on interviews made in 1997 with Aurovilians who lived here between 1968 and 1973. The interviews presented in this book are part of a history program for newcomers that I had created with my friend, Philip Melville in 1997. The plan was to divide Auroville's history into different eras and then interview Aurovilians according to their area of knowledge.

Our first section would cover the years from 1968 till 1973 when the Mother was still in her physical body.

The Way of the Sunlit Path

May The Way of the Sunlit Path be a convenient guide for activating this ancient truth as a support for a Conscious Evolution.
May it illumine the transformation offered to us in the Integral Yoga.

A Dream Takes Shape (in English, French, Hindi)

A comprehensive brochure on the international township of Auroville in, ranging from its Charter and "Why Auroville?" to the plan of the township, the central Matrimandir, the national pavilions and residences, to working groups, the economy, making visits, how to join, its relationship to the Sri Aurobindo Ashram, and its key role in the future of the world. This brochure endeavours to highlight how The Mother envisioned Auroville from its inception, some of the major achievements realised over the years, and some of the difficulties currently faced in implementing the guidelines which she gave.

Mother on Japan

I had everything to learn in Japan. For four years, from an artistic point of view, I lived from wonder to wonder. And everything in this city, in this country, from beginning to end, gives you the impression of impermanence, of the unexpected, the exceptional... ...everything in this city, in this country, from beginning to end, gives you the impression of impermanence, of the unexpected, the exceptional. You always come to things you did not expect; you want to find them again and they are lost – they have made something else which is equally charming.

Auroville Reflected

On 28 February 1968, on an impoverished plateau on the Coromandel Coast of South India, about 4,000 people from around the world gathered for a most unusual inauguration. Handfuls of soil from the countries of the world were mixed together as a symbol of human unity. Why did Indira Gandhi, the erstwhile Prime Minister of India, support this development for "a city the earth needs?" Why did UNESCO endorse this project? Why does the Dalai Lama continue to be involved in the project? What led anthropologist Margaret Mead to insist that records must be kept of its progress? Why did both historian William Irwin Thompson and United Nations representative Robert Muller note that this social experiment may be a breakthrough for humanity even as critics commented, "it is an impossible dream"?

A House For the Third Millennium
Essays on Matrimandir

Nightwatch at the Matrimandir...
A cosmic spectacle; the black expanse above, the big black crater of Matrimandir's excavation carved deep into the soil. The four pillars - two of which are completed and the other two nearing completion - are four huge ships coming together from the four corners of the earth to meet at this pro propitious spot...

Passage to More than India

This book is a voyage of discovery. In 1959 the author, Dick Batstone, a classically educated bookseller in England, with a Christian background, comes across a life of the great Indian polymath Sri Aurobindo, though a series of apparently fortuitous circumstances. A meeting in Durham, England, leads him to a determination to get to the Sri Aurobindo Ashram in Pondicherry, a former French territory south of Madras.

www.ingramcontent.com/pod-product-compliance
Lightning Source LLC
LaVergne TN
LVHW010323070526
838199LV00065B/5642